BEYOND the Screen

RESILIENT KIDS IN A DIGITAL WORLD

Jason Daniels, PhD

innovativeink PUBLISHING
A Division of Kendall Hunt

Cover image Shutterstock.com

innovativeink
PUBLISHING
A Division of Kendall Hunt

www.innovativeinkpublishing.com
Send all inquiries to:
4050 Westmark Drive
Dubuque, IA 52004-1840

Print ISBN: 979-8-3851-3035-1
eBook ISBN: 979-8-3851-3036-8

Published in the United States of America

Contents

Introduction: Why This Book Matters

If you're a parent today, you're raising your child in a world that looks *completely different from* the one you grew up in. Remember waiting all week for Saturday morning cartoons or spending entire summers outside because your parents told you to "go play"? If you were lucky, maybe you had a Game Boy — and even that felt high-tech. Road trips? Endless hours of staring out the window, inventing games to fight boredom.

Fast forward to today: our kids have instant, 24/7 access to content YouTube, TikTok, video games, AI toys, streaming shows all just a tap away. Conversations? More likely through a screen than face-to-face.

Yes, digital media can allow for creativity, is often convenient, and can even help us stay connected. But it also comes with distractions, disconnection, and many about what it's doing to our kids and our families.

You may be asking:

- How much screen time is too much?
- Will constant exposure affect their brain development?
- How can I stop my child from melting down when I turn the tablet/video game off?
- How do I raise a child who's both technologically literate and emotionally regulated?

This book grew out of the questions I've asked — and the countless ones I've been asked by parents navigating the digital world with their kids. As a developmental psychologist, educator, and parent, I've spent years studying how digital media impacts children's learning, relationships, and mental well-being.

But I've also lived it. I've negotiated screen time limits during Minecraft meltdowns. I've watched teens wrestle with their self-worth after scrolling through social media. And yes — I've sat at the dinner table, trying to have a meaningful, device-free conversation... while someone's phone buzzed in the background (sometimes mine).

I've come to realize through my research and real life that parenting in the digital age isn't about getting everything right. It's about asking good questions, staying curious, and making intentional choices that align with what matters to our families.

Here's the good news: you don't need to be a perfect parent to raise healthy, happy, resilient kids in the digital age. Research shows it's not about perfection it's about being present, responsive, and intentional.

Sure, childhood today looks different than it did when we were growing up. But different isn't always bad — sometimes it's just new. The development of digital media has created amazing opportunities for learning, creativity, and connection. I've found how-to videos to fix leaky faucets, discovered new recipes, and even learned things I wish I'd known back in school. And our kids? They're using those same tools to explore, express themselves, and connect with the world around them.

We don't need to ditch technology — we just need to guide our children on how to use it effectively. Research supports the idea that when adults set thoughtful boundaries and model healthy habits, kids are more likely to develop balanced digital lives. It's not about saying "no" to screens — it's about helping our kids say "yes" to what really matters and making deliberate, mindful choices about who and when to use technology.

This book will help you:

- Understand how digital media affects your child's development
- Set realistic boundaries without constant battles
- Promote critical thinking and digital literacy
- Create a home environment where real-life connections can flourish
- Model healthy digital habits yourself

Whether your child is just learning to hold a tablet or about to head off to college, this book offers age-appropriate, practical strategies rooted in research and tested in real-life parenting.

This isn't about fear, guilt, or shame. It's about giving you the tools and confidence to parent with purpose in a digital world. Because yes — it *is* possible to raise kids who can thrive with technology without being consumed by it.

With the right knowledge and a little intentionality, you can help your child develop healthy habits, strong relationships, and a balanced sense of self — both online and off. With recent research showing that teens spend an average of nearly 9 hours a day on screens, there's never been a more important time to guide their digital journey with care.

References

Center on the Developing Child at Harvard University. (2015). *Brain architecture, early experiences, and toxic stress.* Center on the Developing Child at Harvard University website. https://developingchild.harvard.edu/resources/wp3/

Christakis, D. A. (2009). The effects of infant media on cognitive development. *Acta Paediatrica, 98*(1), 8–16.

Common Sense Media. (2022). *The Common Sense Census: Media use by tweens and teens, 2021.* Common Sense Media. https://www.commonsensemedia.org/research/the-common-sense-census-media-use-by-tweens-and-teens-2021

Rideout, V. (2017). *The Common Sense Census: Media use by kids age zero to eight, 2017.* Common Sense Media. https://www.commonsensemedia.org/research/the-common-sense-census-media-use-by-kids-age-zero-to-eight-2017

Rideout, V., & Robb, M. B. (2019). *The Common Sense Census: Media use by tweens and teens, 2019.* Common Sense Media. https://www.commonsensemedia.org/research/the-common-sense-census-media-use-by-tweens-and-teens-2019

Swing, E. L., Gentile, D. A., Anderson, C. A., & Shiflett, D. (2010). Television and video game exposure and the development of attention problems. *Pediatrics, 126*(2), 214–221.

1

Digital Childhood

"They're like little tech ninjas — swiping, scrolling, tapping — before they even learn to talk." *Tristan Harris*

If you've ever watched a toddler unlock a phone, open an app, and start playing like it's second nature, you've seen how much childhood has changed. These screen-savvy kids aren't following instructions; they're engaging with technology designed to feel effortless from the very first touch, even for the youngest users. And that's by design.

Touchscreens, autoplay, and endless scrolls are built to hold attention, often longer than we'd like. When I first started researching digital media, I was focused on the contrast between online and offline behavior. But today's kids? They don't see that line. They're growing up in a world where digital and real life are completely intertwined — where "online" isn't a destination, it's just part of the everyday. For many of us, there isn't an offline world anymore… unless we intentionally create one.

This constant connection to technology from a young age, significantly impacts how children form attachments. Attachment theory reveals how deep emotional bonds children form with caregivers influence their behavior and relationships. Secure attachments in early childhood foster healthy emotional development, and these bonds often shape how children seek and engage with the world around them, including with digital media.

With the rise of digital media, children are increasingly exposed to content that competes with caregivers for their attention. This may not seem like a problem at first glance but consider the role of attachment in early development: secure attachments provide the foundation for emotional regulation, attention span, and the ability to focus on one thing at a time. When children's attention is constantly pulled by devices designed to be ever engaging, it may interfere with their ability to form these healthy emotional bonds, both with people and their environments.

And considering that children under 8 now spend an average of 2.5 hours a day on screens — often before they've even learned to read — it's clear we need to start thinking critically about the role technology plays in their development. Attachment forms the basis for how children respond to their digital interactions, and understanding this connection will be key to later chapters, where we'll explore how digital media impacts attachment and the long-term implications of these early experiences.

We've crossed into uncharted territory. This is the first generation of kids to:

- Use touch screens before they can hold a pencil
- Learn letters through apps instead of books
- Have a digital footprint before they take their first steps
- Navigate social relationships through likes, snaps, and emojis

While past generations worried about how much TV was too much, today's parents are navigating an entire digital ecosystem — tablets, smartphones, gaming consoles, smart TVs, educational apps, virtual reality, smartwatches and rings, and even AI-powered tools. Technology isn't just a part of life anymore — it's woven into every corner of it: home, school, friendships, family time... even bedtime and sleep routines.

What Does This Mean for Development?

One of the most common questions parents ask me is, *"Is all this screen time changing my kid's brain?"* And the short answer is — yes. That's called learning.

Every experience we have shapes the brain, and during childhood, especially in the first few years, the brain is incredibly malleable. Neural connections form at a rapid pace, influenced by everything a child interacts with, people, objects, and yes, also screens. But not all screen time is created equal.

Think of it like this: passive screen time, such as scrolling through social media or watching videos, is often a one-way interaction. The brain is absorbing information, but it's not engaging deeply with it. Active screen time, in contrast, such as playing an interactive game, engaging with an educational app, or using technology for a creative project requires more involvement. It can promote problem-solving, encourage critical thinking, and help build social skills.

Both active and passive screen time shape the developing brain, but not equally, and both come with trade-offs. Research shows that active engagement with digital media such as interactive games or problem-solving apps — offers more cognitive and social benefits than passive consumption, like watching videos or scrolling through feeds.

Still, even high-quality digital engagement cannot match the developmental value of real-world experiences. Face-to-face conversations, physical play, and hands-on collaboration provide richer opportunities for developing language, empathy, attention, and coordination — the kinds of learning that screens, no matter how engaging, cannot replicate.

While some screen time can be educational and support skill development, screen time needs to be balanced with experiences that involve movement, direct social interaction, and creative exploration. These offline activities help children build motor skills, emotional intelligence, and nuanced social awareness by interpreting facial expressions, body language, and tone of voice in real time.

By age three, a child's brain is creating more than one million new neural connections per second. Every interaction — whether with a screen, a book, or a toy — contributes to this rapid brain development. But the real question isn't whether digital media has an impact rather, the question is, can shape that impact to support healthy, whole-child development?

The Double-Edged Nature of Digital Media

While digital tools can support creativity, connection, and learning, they can also present challenges when used excessively or without balance. Understanding how digital media can both help and hinder development is key to using it in ways that protect and promote children's overall well-being.

HOW DOES DIGITAL MEDIA SUPPORT DEVELOPMENT?

- Educational games can serve as effective tools for enhancing language and math skills. Studies have demonstrated that game-based learning programs can significantly improve students' math problem-solving abilities and motivation compared to traditional instructional methods. Similarly, digital games have been shown to aid in developing reading skills among young learners.
- Video chats offer a valuable means for children to maintain connections with distant family members and friends, particularly when in-person interactions

are not feasible. Research indicates that video chat supports word young children's learning and social-emotional development. The contingent nature of video chats—allowing for real-time, responsive communication—makes them uniquely beneficial among digital media.

- Interactive apps can stimulate children's curiosity and creativity. Engaging with apps that incorporate interactive elements, such as drawing, building virtual structures, or solving puzzles, can foster exploration and critical thinking. Furthermore, digital game-based learning applications have been found to improve creativity skills in preschool children.

HOW DOES DIGITAL MEDIA HINDER DEVELOPMENT?

- Overstimulation from excessive screen time can reduce attention span. Fast-paced videos and games that rapidly shift focus can train young brains to expect constant novelty, making it harder for them to concentrate on tasks requiring sustained attention. Research indicates that children exposed to more screen time at ages 3 to 5 exhibit decreased organization in brain regions responsible for attention, visual processing, and language, which are crucial for academic skills.

- Screen-based play can displace hands-on exploration, such as building with blocks, drawing, or outdoor play. These activities are vital for developing fine and gross motor skills and offer rich sensory learning experiences that screens can't fully replicate. Studies have found that higher digital-media usage negatively impacts fine motor skill development in preschool children, as the repetitive tasks associated with screen use do not stimulate motor development to the same degree as hands-on experiences.

- Passive media like watching TV or scrolling through social media—can delay the development of language and social skills. Children learn best through active engagement with their environment and other people. Excessive and unsupervised passive digital media use has been linked to speech delays, with later introduction of digital devices correlating with better language development.

- Digital media use can interrupt caregiver-child interactions, which are crucial for socialization and emotional development. When parents and children are distracted by screens, opportunities for meaningful face-to-face conversations and play diminish. Research shows that parental distractions, including digital media use, can disrupt the quality and quantity of interactions between parents and toddlers, negatively affecting the child's social and emotional development.

THE BOTTOM LINE?

The impact of digital media isn't all good or all bad. It depends on what's being used, how much, how often, and whether it's replacing essential developmental experiences like play, sleep, conversation, and physical movement. When technology is used mindfully and balanced with other activities, it can be a valuable tool in supporting children's growth. But when it takes over and crowds out the real-world experiences that children need to thrive, that's when it can become a problem.

Digital Milestones: What Kids Are Doing (and When)

Every stage of childhood brings its own digital behaviors — and challenges. Here are some examples of what you can expect at each age:

AGES 0–2

Babies and toddlers may be starring in those adorable photos on social media, but their screen time is still mostly parent-controlled. At this age, digital interactions are limited, and there's little evidence that children under 2 can learn from screens. The main risks? Overexposure to digital media and a lack of face-to-face interaction with caregivers and peers, are crucial for early development.

AGES 3–5

Welcome to touchscreen mastery! At this stage, kids are likely to spend a lot of time playing games and watching videos. The challenges here are real: tantrums when devices are taken away and developing habits that can be difficult to break as they get older. Setting limits early on is key but expect some pushback!

AGES 6–9

Kids may get their own devices (or borrow yours), and they start to explore online games, YouTube™, and digital tools for school. The risks at this age are exposure to inappropriate content and early peer pressure, as kids become more aware of social media and online trends. It's a time when digital supervision needs to ramp up.

AGES 10–13

As kids become more independent, their curiosity about social media starts to grow. They begin forming a digital identity — posting, sharing, and engaging online. The challenges here are significant: they are more vulnerable to online influence and the emotional ups and downs that often come with social media use.

AGES 14–17

Digital life becomes social life. Texting, posting, streaming, and gaming dominate their daily routines. The risks at this stage are more pronounced: digital media addiction, comparison culture, and online drama. Teens are navigating more complex social dynamics online, and it's crucial to keep communication open and ensure they're using their digital lives in a healthy way.

Table1 - Digital Milestones by Age

Age Range	Typical Digital Behaviors	Developmental Considerations	Key Risks	Parental Tips
0–2	Watching videos with caregivers, video chats	Limited learning from screens; needs face-to-face interaction	Overstimulation, delayed language	Avoid solo screen time; focus on interaction
3–5	Playing simple games, touchscreen use	Developing habits, early self-regulation	Tantrums, poor transitions	Set short, consistent limits
6–9	Online gaming, school-related screen use	Beginning to explore online identity	Exposure to inappropriate content	Monitor usage, use filters
10–13	Social media curiosity; content creation	Identity development, peer influence	Social pressure, screen dependence	Encourage conversations about content
14–17	Heavy social media, gaming	Peer validation, self-worth linked to screens	Mental health, addiction	Set boundaries, co-create tech rules

The Digital Avalanche

If you're feeling overwhelmed by the impact of the digital world on both you and your kids, you're not alone. One moment, your child is quietly watching a video or playing with an app while you get dinner ready. Next, you're concerned they're caught up in endless scrolling. You might have tried setting limits, only to face arguments, tears, or even silence. It can feel like you're constantly trying to keep up with an ever-moving digital tide.

Here's the thing: the key isn't to try to eliminate digital media completely — that's both unrealistic and unnecessary. It's like trying to hold back an avalanche. The real goal is to help your child build a healthy relationship with technology, one that supports their development, safeguards their well-being, and strengthens the bond you share. By learning how to regulate digital use together, you'll both gain the tools needed to navigate the digital world in a way that benefits your family, not overwhelms it.

In the Next Chapter...

In the next chapter, we're going to dig into the benefits and risks of digital media — and don't worry, this isn't about scaring or guilting you! It's about giving you the clarity you need to make confident, informed choices as a parent. You'll learn what the latest research really says and how to find that sweet spot of balance in your home, so you can guide your kids' digital use in a way that supports their growth and well-being.

References

American Academy of Pediatrics Council on Communications and Media. (2016). Media and young minds. Pediatrics, 138(5), e20162591. https://doi.org/10.1542/peds.2016-2591

Christakis, D. A. (2009). The effects of infant media on cognitive development. Acta Paediatrica, 98(1), 8–16. https://doi.org/10.1111/j.1651-2227.2008.01027.x

Common Sense Media. (2022). The Common Sense Census: Media use by tweens and teens, 2021. Common Sense Media. https://www.commonsensemedia.org/research/the-common-sense-census-media-use-by-tweens-and-teens-2021

Common Sense Media. (2017). The Common Sense Census: Media use by kids age zero to eight, 2017. Common Sense Media. https://www.commonsensemedia.org/research/the-common-sense-census-media-use-by-kids-age-zero-to-eight-2017

Common Sense Media. (2019). The Common Sense Census: Media use by tweens and teens, 2019. Common Sense Media. https://www.commonsensemedia.org/research/the-common-sense-census-media-use-by-tweens-and-teens-2019

Horowitz-Kraus, T., & Hutton, J. S. (2018). Brain connectivity in children is increased by the time they spend reading books and decreased by the length of exposure to screen-based media. Acta Paediatrica, 107(4), 685–693. https://doi.org/10.1111/apa.14176

McClure, E., Chentsova-Dutton, Y., Barr, R., Holochwost, S. J., & Parrott, W. G. (2015). "Facetime doesn't count": Video chat as an exception to media restrictions for infants and toddlers. International Journal of Child-Computer Interaction, 6, 1–6. https://doi.org/10.1016/j.ijcci.2016.02.002

Radesky, J. S., Schumacher, J., & Zuckerman, B. (2015). Mobile and interactive media use by young children: The good, the bad, and the unknown. Pediatrics, 135(1), 1–3. https://doi.org/10.1542/peds.2014-2251

Rideout, V. (2017). The Common Sense Census: Media use by kids age zero to eight, 2017. Common Sense Media. https://www.commonsensemedia.org/research/the-common-sense-census-media-use-by-kids-age-zero-to-eight-2017

Rideout, V., & Robb, M. B. (2019). The Common Sense Census: Media use by tweens and teens, 2019. Common Sense Media. https://www.commonsensemedia.org/research/the-common-sense-census-media-use-by-tweens-and-teens-2019

Swing, E. L., Gentile, D. A., Anderson, C. A., & Shiflett, D. (2010). Television and video game exposure and the development of attention problems. Pediatrics, 126(2), 214–221. https://doi.org/10.1542/peds.2009-1508

Zimmerman, F. J., Christakis, D. A., & Meltzoff, A. N. (2007). Associations between media viewing and language development in children under age 2 years. The Journal of Pediatrics, 151(4), 364–368. https://doi.org/10.1016/j.jpeds.2007.04.071

2

The Good, the Bad, and the Addictive

"Not all screen time is created equal. And not all tech use is toxic."
Dr. Patrice A. Harris, MD, MA

It's easy to feel guilty as a parent, when we compare ourselves to others and feel like we're not measuring up. Many of us worry that letting our kids play video games or spend time on their devices means we're somehow failing. But here's the thing: guilt, while it can motivate change, usually just leaves us feeling bad without actually helping. So, it's time to let go of that guilt.

For most of us, digital media itself isn't the problem — it's how it's used. Digital media can fuel creativity, enhance learning, and help kids stay connected with others. But it can also overwhelm them, cause isolation, and overstimulate their brains. The important thing isn't to eliminate it altogether — it's to understand the risks and to learn how to use it wisely.

In this chapter, we'll explore both the benefits and the risks of digital media, giving you the knowledge you need to make informed, confident decisions that align with your child's needs — not based on fear or the latest trends.

The Good: When Digital Media Supports Development

Digital media isn't inherently good or bad; it's how we use it that makes the difference. When used intentionally, in moderation, and with guidance, digital media can be a powerful tool for enhancing a child's development. Here's how:

ACCESS TO LEARNING

Educational apps, videos, and interactive platforms can help reinforce early literacy, numeracy, and science concepts. When children engage with well-designed educational technology, they can improve reading and math skills. For example, apps that focus on letter recognition, counting, or math games can offer engaging, personalized learning experiences that help solidify foundational knowledge.

Beyond academics, children can use technology to explore the world and beyond, virtually — from the vastness of the solar system to the wonders of ocean life. Virtual field trips, interactive science experiments, and documentary-style videos are just a few ways technology makes learning more dynamic. Research by the Pew Research Center also found that when digital media is used for exploration, it can spark a child's natural curiosity, leading to more self-directed learning and discovery.

Many platforms incorporate gamification—the use of game elements like rewards, levels, and points—to make learning feel fun and rewarding. This strategy can significantly boost engagement and retention, as it taps into the brain's reward systems; gamification increases motivation by turning tasks into challenges and rewarding progress.

CREATIVITY AND EXPRESSION

Digital media tools allow children to express themselves in new ways. Kids can draw, make music, code, build digital worlds, and even create animations or podcasts. These platforms provide a rich space for self-expression and creativity, offering more than traditional pencil-and-paper activities can.

Popular games like Minecraft™ and Roblox™ (when used in moderation) encourage open-ended exploration and problem-solving. Both platforms promote creativity by allowing children to design their own structures, landscapes, and experiences. In fact, research shows that platforms like these can foster critical thinking, collaboration, and resilience, as children work through problems, navigate social interactions, and try new ideas in a safe virtual environment.

CONNECTION WITH OTHERS

In the digital age, staying connected has never been simpler. Video calls allow children to maintain relationships with distant family and friends, especially when geographical distances or health restrictions might make in-person visits challenging. Research has shown that video calls can improve emotional connection and social bonding, especially for children who are separated from family members.

Shared online games offer a valuable opportunity for social interaction and friendship-building. For children who may be shy or neurodivergent, these games provide a low-pressure environment where they can practice communication and collaboration. Multiplayer games encourage teamwork, empathy, and the development of social skills, creating an inclusive space where children of all abilities can connect and interact.

SUPPORT FOR DIVERSE LEARNERS

Digital media can be a lifeline for children with learning differences or disabilities. Many educational tools come with accessibility features like text-to-speech, closed captions, and customizable learning environments, which can support kids with learning disabilities or sensory challenges. For example, children with dyslexia may benefit from apps that read text aloud, while children with ADHD might find that interactive tools help maintain their focus.

Digital media tools have been shown to significantly enhance learning experiences for students, particularly those with learning disabilities. These tools can be tailored to meet individual learning styles, providing opportunities for personalized instruction that helps children with diverse needs thrive academically. Many educators report that digital technologies improve student engagement and skills, allowing for greater academic success, because the tools can be adapted to the needs of each learner. The flexibility of digital media can allow for a more inclusive, responsive learning environment.

The Bad: When Screens Displace What Matters Most

As compelling as digital media can be, problems arise when it takes the place of experiences that are essential for healthy development — like sleep, physical activity, play, and face-to-face interaction. Here's where things can start to go off track:

DELAYED LANGUAGE AND SOCIAL SKILLS

For young children, face-to-face interaction is critical for developing language and social skills. When kids spend too much time passively watching digital screens, they miss out on essential back-and-forth conversations with caregivers and peers. This is where much of their early language learning happens.

Children under the age of 2 who spend excessive time in front of digital screens are less likely to develop the vocabulary and social skills they need to thrive. It's not just about talking — it's about the back-and-forth interaction, which builds the neural pathways for language development. Passive screen use reduces these opportunities, leading to delays in both language and social growth.

DISRUPTED SLEEP

When kids use digital media too close to bedtime, it can interfere with their sleep cycle. While the blue light emitted from their screens suppresses the production of melatonin, the hormone that regulates sleep, making it harder for children to fall asleep, it's also the increased mental and emotional stimulation from interactive content that contributes to this disruption. Studies, including one from Harvard

Medical School, show that children who engage in screen time before bed experience delayed sleep onset and lower sleep quality. This disruption can affect mood, attention, and overall well-being the next day.

Sleep is critical for brain development, emotional regulation, and even memory consolidation. Without enough high-quality sleep, children's ability to learn, concentrate, and regulate their emotions can be compromised.

REDUCED PHYSICAL ACTIVITY

It's no surprise that the more time children spend using digital media, the less time they spend moving their bodies. This lack of physical activity can lead to a host of issues, including poor physical health, difficulty with emotional regulation, and impaired concentration.

Children aged 5 to 17 should aim for at least an hour of physical activity each day, but excessive digital media use often crowds out opportunities for movement. Physical activity not only strengthens muscles and bones but also supports brain development and emotional well-being. When kids don't get enough exercise, it can negatively impact their ability to focus, manage stress, and maintain a positive mood.

MENTAL HEALTH CONCERNS

The overuse of digital media — particularly social media and video games — has been linked to increased rates of anxiety, depression, loneliness, and low self-esteem, especially in teens. Social comparison, cyberbullying, and the addictive nature of certain games can exacerbate these issues.

A study published in 2019 found that teens who spent more than three hours a day using digital media were significantly more likely to report mental health concerns. Social media platforms, in particular, have been shown to contribute to feelings of isolation, insecurity, and anxiety as teens compare themselves to curated, idealized versions of others' lives. Video games, while fun, can also contribute to emotional distress when they replace real-world interactions and healthy coping mechanisms.

The Addictive: Why It's So Hard to Put Digital Media Down

Let's face it: the digital world is designed to keep us and our kids coming back for more. It's not just your imagination; this is the result of psychology at work. Tech companies use a range of strategies to keep users engaged, making it increasingly difficult to put down.

INFINITE SCROLL

One of the most common features you'll encounter on social media platforms, video apps, and websites is the infinite scroll — content that never stops coming. There are no "stopping cues" like an end to a chapter or a break for a commercial. As soon as your child finishes one post or video, another one is right there, just waiting for them to watch or interact.

Research shows that this kind of design taps into our brains' desire for novelty and unpredictability, which makes it easier to lose track of time. The endless stream of information doesn't give us the natural stopping points we need to break free.

AUTOPLAY

Another feature that keeps kids glued to their digital devices is autoplay. Whether it's videos on YouTube™ or a new episode of their favorite show, autoplay removes the friction of making a choice about what to watch next. Once one video ends, another automatically starts, which keeps kids engaged without having to think about what to do next.

Autoplay features are designed to capitalize on "decision fatigue," the idea that the more choices we make, the less mental energy we have left to make future decisions. Autoplay eliminates the need for a choice, making it easier for kids to stay engaged longer.

DOPAMINE TRIGGERS: LIKES, STREAKS, AND REWARDS

Have you ever noticed how kids (and even adults) get hooked on likes, streaks, or rewards from social media apps and video games? That's because these features trigger the release of dopamine, the brain's "feel-good" neurotransmitter. Every like, comment, or reward activates the brain's pleasure center, encouraging users to keep engaging in the activity to get more of that pleasurable sensation.

This reward system is the same principle behind habits formed in gambling — each notification or reward is a small "win," which makes your child want to keep scrolling or playing. It creates a cycle of anticipation, reward, and repetition.

PERSONALIZED CONTENT

Perhaps one of the most insidious aspects of modern digital media is personalized content. Social media platforms, video apps, and even educational games are all designed to show users exactly what they're most likely to engage with. These platforms use algorithms to track behavior and then serve up more of the same types of content that will keep your child hooked. Whether it's videos, games, or ads, the content becomes increasingly tailored to your child's preferences, making it harder for them to look away.

The Netflix documentary *The Social Dilemma* (2020), delves into how social media platforms use algorithms to personalize content, thereby increasing user engagement and potentially leading to addictive usage patterns. The film illustrates how these algorithms track user behavior to serve increasingly tailored content, making it harder for users, including children, to disengage.

Even Adults Struggle — So How Can Kids Do It?

It's not just kids who struggle with digital media use. Adults often find it difficult to regulate their own digital habits, whether it's getting lost in social media, binge-watching shows, or playing games for hours. And yet, we expect children, with their still-developing brains and self-regulation skills, to navigate these digital temptations without guidance.

Studies show that adults and children alike can become addicted to the dopamine loop that digital media creates, which is why many apps and games are designed to keep users hooked. According to The American Academy of Pediatrics, the addictive nature of digital media and the challenge of self-regulation can be even more intense for children and teens.

WHY SETTING BOUNDARIES MATTERS

The truth is that many apps and games are built with the intention of keeping your child engaged for as long as possible. Understanding these design strategies is crucial in helping you set healthy boundaries for your child's digital media use. The goal isn't to eliminate digital media entirely, but to teach your child how to navigate the digital world in a way that supports their growth, development, and well-being.

It's not always easy, and it can feel like a battle. But by being aware of the strategies that keep your child hooked, you can work together with your child to create a more balanced relationship with technology.

SO, WHAT SHOULD PARENTS DO?

As parents, the sheer volume of digital media options and recommendations can be overwhelming. It's tempting to get stuck on the question, *"How much screen time is okay?"* However, a, perhaps, more helpful mindset is to understand that not all screen time is created equal. It's not just about the number of hours spent in front of a screen, but about how those hours are spent and how they contribute to your child's overall development.

Instead of focusing solely on limits, ask yourself:

Is it helping or harming my child's development?

Some types of digital media support development — think educational apps, online learning platforms, or creative games that stimulate problem-solving and critical thinking. These can foster skills such as language acquisition, numeracy, and even emotional regulation.

On the other hand, passive media consumption — like mindlessly watching TV or scrolling through social media — can potentially harm development. The key is to identify what types of digital media use are enriching your child's development and what might be detracting from it.

Is it supporting or replacing relationships?

Digital media has the potential to bring people together, but it can also replace valuable in-person interactions. Video calls with distant family members, shared online games, and social media can help your child stay connected with others when physical distance is a barrier.

However, too much time using digital media can displace face-to-face communication, which is essential for building social skills, empathy, and emotional intelligence. According to Sherry Turkle, a professor at MIT and expert on technology's impact on relationships, prolonged digital media use can lead to feelings of isolation, even when children are virtually connected to others. It's important to ask yourself: Is their use of digital media helping foster positive relationships, or is it taking time away from crucial in-person interactions?

Is it adding value or just filling time?

It's easy to let digital media fill the gaps in daily life — whether it's turning on the TV to keep your child occupied or allowing endless YouTube™ videos to pass the time. But what is it adding to your child's life?

Intentional use of digital media can bring value by supporting learning, creativity, and social connection. However, mindless use, like endlessly scrolling through social media or watching unengaging content, is often just a way to kill time without any real benefit. Unstructured, passive media use can lead to negative outcomes, including impaired academic performance and reduced physical activity. Be mindful of how technology is used — does it provide something enriching, or is it simply a way to pass time?

Is it encouraging creativity or passive consumption?

One of the best ways digital media can support your child's development is by encouraging creativity. Platforms like YouTube™, Minecraft™, and apps that allow your child to create their own stories, designs, or games can spark imagination and problem-solving skills. Interactive apps that promote creativity can be particularly beneficial because they engage your child in the learning process.

In contrast, passive consumption such as watching TV shows or mindlessly scrolling through social media encourages little to no engagement. This can have a negative impact on your child's ability to think critically or creatively. Studies show that active engagement with technology where your child is creating, exploring, or interacting is far more beneficial for their cognitive development than passive viewing.

QUALITY OVER QUANTITY

When you shift your focus from *how much screen time* is ok to *how meaningful the screen time is*, you'll start to parent tech use the same way you parent other important areas of your child's life: with intentionality, flexibility, and love. Just like with food, sleep, or behavior, it's not about rigid rules but about balance.

If you make thoughtful decisions based on what benefits your child's development, you can help your child navigate the digital world in a healthy, positive way. Remember, the goal is not to eliminate digital media, but to use it as a tool that complements and enhances the real-life experiences your child needs for growth.

By being intentional about screen time or other digital media use, you can empower your child to make the most of the digital world — while still prioritizing what matters most: relationships, play, creativity, and well-being.

In the Next Chapter…

We'll take a deeper look at mental health in the digital age; how digital media use affects anxiety, mood, and sleep and how you can support your child in developing habits that nurture a calm, connected nervous system in an always-on world.

Because raising a healthy digital kid isn't just about limiting damage — it's about building strength from the inside out.

References

American Academy of Pediatrics. (n.d.). *Center of Excellence on Social Media and Youth Mental Health*. Retrieved from https://www.aap.org/en/patient-care/media-and-children/center-of-excellence-on-social-media-and-youth-mental-health/

American Academy of Pediatrics. (n.d.). *Media and Children*. Retrieved from https://www.aap.org/en/patient-care/media-and-children/

American Academy of Pediatrics. (2016). Media and young minds. Pediatrics, 138(5), e20162591. https://doi.org/10.1542/peds.2016-2591

Anderson, A. A., Brossard, D., Scheufele, D. A., Xenos, M. A., & Ladwig, P. (2014). The "nasty effect:" Online incivility and risk perceptions of emerging technologies. *Journal of Computer-Mediated Communication, 19*(3), 373–387. https://doi.org/10.1111/jcc4.12009

Anderson, D. R., & Subrahmanyam, K. (2017). Digital screen media and cognitive development. Pediatrics, 140(Supplement_2), S57–S61. https://doi.org/10.1542/peds.2016-1758E

Barr, R., & Linebarger, D. N. (Eds.). (2017). Media exposure during infancy and early childhood: The effects of content and context on learning and development. Springer.

Bickham, D. S. (2021). Current research and viewpoints on screen time and children. Pediatrics, 147(2), e2020040273. https://doi.org/10.1542/peds.2020-040273

Choi, Y., Choi, J., & Seering, J. (2025). Leveling Up Together: Fostering Positive Growth and Safe Online Spaces for Teen Roblox Developers. *arXiv*. https://arxiv.org/abs/2502.18120

Christakis, D. A. (2014). Interactive media use at younger than the age of 2 years: Time to rethink the American Academy of Pediatrics guideline? JAMA Pediatrics, 168(5), 399–400. https://doi.org/10.1001/jamapediatrics.2013.5081

Christakis, D. A., Ramirez, J. S. B., Ferguson, S. M., Ravinder, S., & Ramirez, J. M. (2018). How early media exposure may affect cognitive function: A review of results from observations in humans and experiments in mice. Proceedings of the National Academy of Sciences, 115(40), 9851–9858. https://doi.org/10.1073/pnas.1611611114

Deterding, S., Dixon, D., Khaled, R., & Nacke, L. (2011). From game design elements to gamefulness: defining 'gamification'. In *Proceedings of the 2011 annual conference extended abstracts on Human factors in computing systems* (pp. 2425–2434). ACM. https://doi.org/10.1145/1979742.1979575

Ferguson, C. J. (2010). Violent video games and aggression: Causal relationship or bystander? *Journal of Youth and Adolescence, 39*(1), 1–14. https://doi.org/10.1007/s10964-009-9443-8

Ferguson, C. J. (2017). Everything in moderation: Moderate use of screens unassociated with child behavior problems. Psychiatric Quarterly, 88(4), 797–805. https://doi.org/10.1007/s11126-016-9486-3

Granic, I., Lobel, A., & Engels, R. C. M. E. (2014). The benefits of playing video games. American Psychologist, 69(1), 66–78. https://doi.org/10.1037/a0034857

Harvard Medical School. (2012). *Screen time and the brain*. Harvard Health Publishing. Retrieved from https://hms.harvard.edu/news/screen-time-brain

Hébert, C., & Jenson, J. (2020). Teaching with sandbox games: Minecraft, game-based learning, and 21st-century competencies. *Canadian Journal of Learning and Technology, 46*(3). https://doi.org/10.21432/cjlt27990

JAMA Psychiatry. (2019). Association of screen time and depression in adolescents. JAMA Psychiatry. https://jamanetwork.com/journals/jamapsychiatry/fullarticle/2749480

Jones, S. E., Ethier, K. A., Hertz, M., et al. (2023). Mental health, suicidality, and connectedness among high school students during the COVID-19 pandemic — adolescent behaviors and experiences survey, United States, January–June 2021. Morbidity and Mortality Weekly Report: Surveillance Summaries, 72(SS-1), 1–11. https://doi.org/10.15585/mmwr.ss7201a1

Meshi, D., Morawetz, C., & Heekeren, H. R. (2013). Nucleus accumbens response to gains in reputation for the self relative to gains for others predicts social media use. *Frontiers in Human Neuroscience, 7*, 439. https://doi.org/10.3389/fnhum.2013.00439

Montag, C., & Walla, P. (2016). Carpe diem instead of losing your social mind: Beyond digital addiction and why we all suffer from digital overuse. *Cogent Psychology, 3*(1), 1157281. https://doi.org/10.1080/23311908.2016.1157281

National Institutes of Health. (2020, June 26). Too much screen time linked to later developmental delays in toddlers. https://www.nichd.nih.gov/newsroom/news/062620-screen-time

Orlowski, J. (Director). (2020). *The Social Dilemma* [Film]. Exposure Labs. Retrieved from https://en.wikipedia.org/wiki/The_Social_Dilemma

Parents Magazine. (2023). Study shows excessive screen time may cause developmental delays in infants. https://www.parents.com/study-shows-screen-time-harm-in-infants-7814272

Pew Research Center. (2012, November 1). How teens do research in the digital world. https://www.pewresearch.org/internet/2012/11/01/how-teens-do-research-in-the-digital-world

Pew Research Center. (2013, February 28). How teachers are using technology at home and in their classrooms: Part III—Bringing technology into the classroom. Pew Research Center's Internet & American Life Project. https://www.pewresearch.org/internet/2013/02/28/part-iii-bringing-technology-into-the-classroom/

Radesky, J. S., Schumacher, J., & Zuckerman, B. (2015). *Mobile and interactive media use by young children: The good, the bad, and the unknown*. Pediatrics, 135(1), 1–3. https://doi.org/10.1542/peds.2014-2251

Riehm, K. E., Feder, K. A., Tormohlen, K. N., Crum, R. M., & Young, A. S. (2019). Associations Between Time Spent Using Social Media and Internalizing and Externalizing Problems Among US Youth. *JAMA Psychiatry, 76*(12), 1266–1273. https://doi.org/10.1001/jamapsychiatry.2019.2325

Rixen, J., Meinhardt, L. M., Glöckler, M., Ziegenbein, M.-L., & Ziegler, J. (2023). The Loop and Reasons to Break It: Investigating Infinite Scrolling Behaviour in Social Media Applications and Reasons to Stop. *Proceedings of the ACM on Human-Computer Interaction, 7*(MHCI), 1–22. https://doi.org/10.1145/3604275

Sweetser, P., Wyeth, P., & Chalmers, M. (2012). Active versus passive screen time for young children. *Australian & New Zealand Journal of Family Therapy, 33*(2), 179–188. https://doi.org/10.1080/183693911203700413

Tarasuik, J. C., Galligan, R., & Kaufman, J. (2011). Almost being there: Video communication with young children. *PLoS ONE, 6*(2), e17129. https://doi.org/10.1371/journal.pone.0017129

Turkle, S. (2012, April). *Connected, but alone?* [Video]. TED Conferences. https://www.ted.com/talks/sherry_turkle_connected_but_alone

Twenge, J. M., Haidt, J., Blake, A. B., & Campbell, W. K. (2023). U.S. teen mental health trends from 2010 to 2019: The roles of screen time and social media. SSRN. https://doi.org/10.2139/ssrn.4604219

Twenge, J. M., & Campbell, W. K. (2018). Associations between screen time and lower psychological well-being among children and adolescents: Evidence from a population-based study. Preventive Medicine Reports, 12, 271–283. https://doi.org/10.1016/j.pmedr.2018.10.003

UNESCO. (2023). Learning for Empathy. https://www.unesco.org/en/articles/learning-empathy

World Health Organization. (2019). Guidelines on physical activity, sedentary behaviour and sleep for children under 5 years of age. https://www.who.int/publications/i/item/9789241550536

Veraksa, N., Veraksa, A., Gavrilova, M., Bukhalenkova, D., Oshchepkova, E., & Chursina, A. (2021). Short- and long-term effects of passive and active screen time on young children's phonological memory. *Frontiers in Education, 6*, 600687. https://doi.org/10.3389/feduc.2021.600687

World Health Organization. (2019). *Guidelines on physical activity, sedentary behaviour and sleep for children under 5 years of age*. Retrieved from https://www.who.int/publications/i/item/9789241550536

Zimmerman, F. J., Christakis, D. A., & Meltzoff, A. N. (2007). Associations between media viewing and language development in children under age 2 years. Journal of Pediatrics, 151(4), 364–368. https://doi.org/10.1016/j.jpeds.2007.04.071

3

Calm in the Chaos — Supporting Mental Health in a Noisy Digital World

"Digital life isn't just loud — it gets under their skin, into their minds, and deep into their sleep." Chimamanda Ngozi Adichie

Today's children are growing up in an environment where notifications never stop, comparison is constant, and even rest comes with the pressure to "stay connected." It's no wonder rates of anxiety, depression, and sleep disturbance are rising among young people.

And while digital media use isn't the sole cause, it is undeniably a powerful influence, shaping how kids feel, think, and relate to themselves and others. From attention and emotion regulation to sleep and self-worth, digital media use can quietly shape mental health in both helpful and harmful ways.

So, how can we help kids find calm, confidence, and clarity amid all this digital noise?

It starts with awareness — understanding the hidden ways digital media can affect mental well-being — and continues with conscious parenting: building habits, boundaries, and conversations that foster emotional strength in a fast-moving world.

How Digital Media Impacts Mental Health

INFORMATION OVERLOAD

Kids today are exposed to an unprecedented volume of information — from news headlines and viral videos to heated online debates and emotionally charged social media posts. Much of this content is fast-paced, emotionally intense, or lacking in nuance, and it reaches children at younger and younger ages.

Even when they're not actively seeking it out, algorithms can push trending topics — including violence, political unrest, environmental disasters, or social conflict — straight into their feeds. This constant input can overwhelm a child's still-developing nervous system, triggering stress responses that make it harder for them to feel calm, focused, or emotionally secure.

Unlike adults, children and adolescents often lack the cognitive and emotional tools to process complex or distressing information. They may struggle to understand context, detect bias, or distinguish between facts and opinion. As a result, they may absorb what they see at face value, internalizing fear, confusion, or helplessness.

Over time, information overload can lead to:

Heightened anxiety or irritability
The brain remains in a hyper-alert state, making it hard to relax or feel safe.

Sleep disturbances
Exposure to intense or upsetting content before bed can disrupt healthy sleep patterns.

Emotional numbness or shutdown
When overwhelmed, some kids may tune out completely — appearing disengaged or indifferent to cope.

Difficulty concentrating
A brain bombarded with too much input can struggle to prioritize tasks or sustain attention.

To support children, it's important to create a buffer zone between them and the constant noise of the digital world. This might include:

- Setting daily digital media-free times (especially before bed)
- Talking openly about what they're seeing online
- Helping them develop critical thinking skills
- Encouraging breaks for nature, movement, and real-world play

Stage	What's Happening & Why It Matters
1. Constant Digital Input	Kids face nonstop stimulation—scrolling, messaging, gaming, notifications. Their brains remain reactive and overstimulated.
2. Overloaded Brain & Nervous System	Fast, emotional, and constant input keeps the nervous system in fight-or-flight. This lowers tolerance for stress and focus.
3. Anxiety, Sleep Issues, Low Mood	Emotional effects begin: trouble sleeping, irritability, and sadness. Poor sleep and mood interfere with learning and regulation.
4. Compensatory Scrolling or Gaming	Children turn to screens to escape discomfort or boredom. Tech becomes a coping tool rather than a choice.
5. Short-Term Relief → Long-Term Crash	Initial feel-good moments fade fast. Kids become restless or upset when stimulation ends. Offline life feels dull by comparison.
6. Increased Dependency & Reduced Resilience	The brain starts to "need" digital hits. Kids struggle to tolerate boredom or distress without a screen. Their resilience erodes.

COMPARISON CULTURE

Social media offers a never-ending highlight reel of other people's lives. Posts are carefully selected, filtered, and curated to show only the most exciting, attractive, or enviable moments. Even when kids *know* what they're seeing isn't the whole truth, they may still feel "less than" in comparis, driving a range of emotional and psychological effects, including:

Low self-worth

Constant comparison to idealized images and lifestyles can make kids feel like they're not measuring up. Over time, this can erode their self-esteem, particularly during adolescence when identity and confidence are still developing.

Social anxiety

Seeing others constantly engaged in social activities or friendships can heighten fears of exclusion or not fitting in. Kids may feel pressure to present themselves perfectly online or worry excessively about how others perceive them, both online and offline.

Perfectionism

Exposure to seemingly "flawless" content can create unrealistic expectations about what success, beauty, or happiness should look like. This may lead to perfectionist thinking — the belief that anything less than ideal is a failure — which can contribute to stress, procrastination, and burnout.

FOMO (Fear of Missing Out)

When kids see peers hanging out without them, or living lives that seem more exciting, it can trigger feelings of being left out or behind. FOMO can lead to compulsive checking of social media and a sense of disconnection from real-life relationships.

The curated nature of social media isn't just misleading — it's emotionally powerful. Helping kids understand how content is crafted and encouraging them to reflect critically on how it affects their thoughts and emotions is an important step in building resilience in the digital age. Media literacy, empathy, and open conversations can go a long way in counteracting the negative effects of constant comparison.

PARENT TIP: HELPING KIDS NAVIGATE THE SOCIAL MEDIA HIGHLIGHT REEL

You can't control everything your child sees online, but you *can* give them the tools to think critically and stay grounded in who they are. Here are a few ways to help:

Talk openly about what "curated" means

Help your child understand that social media is like a movie trailer — it shows the best parts, not the whole story. Ask questions like, *"What do you think might be happening behind that photo?"* or *"Do you think this post reflects their everyday life?"*

Encourage "reality checks"

Share examples of your own filtered vs. unfiltered moments (when appropriate) to show that it's normal for life to be messy or imperfect. This helps to normalize real emotions and real experiences.

Limit passive scrolling time

Encourage your child to take breaks from endless scrolling. Instead, guide them toward creative or interactive uses of digital media, like making music, designing graphics, or video chatting with friends.

Model self-compassion

Talk about your challenges and how you handle self-doubt or comparison. Our children can learn a lot from how we manage our own emotions, especially in a digital media-driven world.

Check in without judgment

Ask open-ended questions like, *"How do you feel after spending time on social media today?"* or *"Have you ever seen something online that made you feel left out?"* The goal is to listen, not lecture.

Promote offline confidence

Make space for your child to develop confidence in real-world settings. Sports, art, volunteering, and unstructured play are potent antidotes to the pressures of online life.

DOPAMINE LOOPS AND EMOTIONAL CRASHES

Many digital apps, especially those designed for entertainment or social media, are built around reward systems that target the brain's dopamine circuitry. Dopamine, a neurotransmitter associated with motivation, reward, and pleasure. It spikes when we anticipate a reward, such as a new like, a game level-up, or the next entertaining video in an endless scroll.

These apps often use features like:

- "Like" buttons and reaction emojis
- Autoplay and infinite scroll
- Streaks and achievements in games
- Surprise-based rewards (loot boxes, pop-ups)

Together, these elements create what's known as a dopamine loop — a cycle where the brain is constantly seeking the next hit of stimulation. And while these micro-rewards can feel exciting in the moment, they don't provide deep or lasting satisfaction.

When the stimulation stops — when the screen turns off, the app is closed, or the rewards don't arrive — children may experience a kind of emotional crash. Their mood can quickly shift to:

- **Irritability**: The sudden absence of stimulation leaves them feeling agitated or short-tempered.
- **Restlessness or boredom**: Offline activities may seem dull by comparison, making it harder to focus on reading, schoolwork, or unstructured play.

- **Emotional withdrawal**: Some kids may become quiet, distant, or even apathetic when the dopamine-driven stimulation ends.

- **Increased digital media-seeking behavior**: Like with sugar or other quick-reward systems, the brain starts to crave more, leading to compulsive checking or difficulty stopping.

While dopamine is a normal and necessary part of healthy development and learning, constant artificial triggering by digital media can create imbalances, most significantly in still-developing brains. This doesn't mean digital media should be avoided altogether — but it does mean kids need support in:

- Recognizing how certain apps make them feel afterward

- Learning to tolerate moments of boredom and rest

- Finding pleasure in slower, more grounded activities like art, nature, play, and in-person connection

SLEEP DISRUPTION

Blue light emitted from our beloved digital screens, smartphones, tablets, and laptops, directly suppresses the release of melatonin, the body's natural signal that it's time to wind down and prepare for sleep. Now, layer on the common practice of late-night scrolling through social media feeds, news articles, or engaging in intense texting conversations. This not only bombards our eyes with sleep-disrupting blue light but also introduces a potent cocktail of emotional stimulation.

That engaging post might spark excitement, a heated debate in the comments could trigger frustration, or even just the sheer volume of information can keep our minds racing. Combine this physiological suppression of melatonin with this heightened state of mental and emotional arousal, and the consequences become clear:

- **Delayed bedtimes**: Our bodies aren't receiving the proper signals to feel sleepy, and our minds are actively engaged, pushing our natural sleep window later and later.

- **Shortened sleep duration**: By the time we finally do manage to fall asleep, the night is already significantly shorter, leaving us with fewer hours of crucial rest.
- **Increased rumination**: The unresolved thoughts and emotions stirred up by late-night digital media use often linger, leading to repetitive worrying and difficulty shutting off our minds once we're in bed.
- **Lower quality, less restorative rest**: Even the sleep we do get is often fragmented and less deep. Our brains haven't had the chance to fully transition into the deeper stages of sleep that are essential for physical and mental restoration.

The cumulative effect of this chronic sleep disruption extends far beyond just feeling tired; sleep loss affects everything:

- **Mood:** We become more irritable, anxious, and prone to emotional reactivity.
- **Attention**: Our focus, concentration, and decision-making abilities are significantly impaired.
- **Learning**: The consolidation of memories and the ability to learn new information are compromised.
- **Physical health**: Chronic sleep deprivation is linked to a higher risk of various health issues, including weakened immune function, weight gain, cardiovascular problems, and metabolic disorders.
- **Emotional resilience**: Our capacity to cope with stress and regulate our emotions is diminished, making us more vulnerable to the challenges of daily life.

The Modern Nervous System: Always On, Rarely at Rest

Every ping, swipe, and alert sends a signal to your child's brain: *pay attention now*. The nervous system, constantly activated, can struggle to return to baseline. Over time, this contributes to chronic stress showing up as mood swings, anxiety, trouble focusing, or emotional outbursts.

Helping kids develop strong nervous systems isn't about removing every digital device. It's about helping them reset and regulate through rest, reflection, and real-world experiences that support emotional safety and balance.

HELPING YOUR CHILD BUILD EMOTIONAL STRENGTH

1. Make Mental Health a Normal Conversation

Inquire about their feelings with the same straightforwardness you use when discussing physical health.

- Instead of just noticing when they are stressed, consider asking them, *"What strategies help you find calm when you feel overwhelmed?"* like asking, *"What do you usually do to soothe a sore muscle?"*
- If you notice them mindlessly or passively scrolling, consider asking them, *"How does using your phone like that make your brain feel?"* like asking, *"What kind of physical activity tends to leave you feeling drained rather than energized?"*
- Instead of beating around the bush, consider asking, *"What emotions are you experiencing right now?"* like asking, *"Are you feeling any aches or pains?"*
- Normalize rest, breaks, therapy, movement, and encourage them to say no to things that feel too much.

2. Create Tech-Free Zones for Mental Rest

Design small parts of the day or space where your child can recharge without digital noise:

- Screen-free mornings or meals
- Device-free bedrooms
- Nature time on weekends
- Family quiet time after dinner

3. Teach Emotional Regulation, Not Suppression

When an experience leaves your child upset, guide them gently:

- Name the emotion: *"You seem frustrated — want to talk?"*
- Offer co-regulation: *"Let's go outside for a few minutes together."*
- Avoid shame: *"Everyone gets overwhelmed sometimes."*

4. Help Them Curate a Healthier Digital Diet

Just like food, the digital content your child consumes affects how they feel. Help them reflect:

- *"What pages or people make you feel stressed or drained?"*
- *"Who makes you laugh or feel seen?"*
- *"Would you feel better muting or unfollowing that account?"*
- Encourage them to be intentional about their feeds — and to notice what lifts or lowers their energy.

TRY THIS AT HOME: "NERVOUS SYSTEM CHECK-INS"

Once or twice a week, invite your child to check in with their body and mind. Ask:

- *"What feels loud or heavy in your mind?"*
- *"What helps you feel calmer and more grounded?"*
- *"When do you feel most peaceful, and what's happening in that moment?"*

Work together to make a personal "calm tools" list — like deep breathing, art, nature, pets, music, or time alone — and post it somewhere visible. These become go-to tools for stressful moments.

When to Worry: Sign0s That May Signal Mental Health Struggles

While mood swings and digital media fatigue are common, certain patterns may suggest a deeper concern:

- Sudden drop in motivation or joy
- Avoidance of real-life social interaction
- Sleep issues (difficulty falling or staying asleep)
- Panic when separated from devices
- Isolation, hopeless talk, or emotional numbness

Trust your instincts. If something feels off, reach out to a counselor, pediatrician, or mental health professional. Early support can make a world of difference — and your calm, non-judgmental presence can be the bridge your child needs.

Table 2 - Warning signs vs Normal Behavior

Behavior	Likely Normal Use	Possible Warning Sign
Screen attachment	Enjoys their favorite app or game	Panic or aggression when a device is removed
Social media use	Chats with friends after school	Obsessive checking, anxiety about posts
Gaming	Plays for fun, takes breaks	Neglects responsibilities, plays to escape stress
Sleep habits	Occasionally stays up watching videos	Persistent insomnia, late-night scrolling
Emotional reactions	Brief frustration over time limits	Major meltdowns, shutdowns, withdrawal

Final Thought: Building Strength from the Inside Out

Supporting mental health in a digital age isn't just about cutting digital media use, it's about nurturing emotional resilience. It's about teaching your child how to listen to their body, recognize their limits, and find grounding even when the world around them is buzzing.

In a culture that glorifies being busy and constantly connected, helping your child slow down, tune in, and breathe may be the most powerful gift you give.

In the Next Chapter...

The next chapter will explore the crucial element of connection in childhood development, particularly in an age increasingly dominated by technology. As parents, maintaining an emotional bond with our children is paramount, yet the pervasive presence of digital media can create a sense of disconnection. This chapter will provide strategies to navigate this complex landscape, focusing on how to preserve and strengthen your emotional connection with your child amidst the digital age. We will delve into establishing healthy boundaries around technology use and explore ways to intentionally leverage technology to support, rather than supplant, meaningful interactions. If you're grappling with the challenge of balancing connection and screen time, know that you're not alone.

References

American Academy of Pediatrics. (2017). Digital media and anxiety and depression in children. Pediatrics, 140(Supplement 2), S76–S80. https://doi.org/10.1542/peds.2016-1758G

Chronobiology in Medicine. (2023). Blue light exposure. Chronobiology in Medicine. https://www.chronobiologyinmedicine.org/journal/view.php?number=167

Jacobs Ladder Group. (2025). The dopamine cycle: Impacts of excessive screen time. https://thejacobsladdergroup.org/2025/04/the-dopamine-cycle-impacts-of-excessive-screen-time

Lembke, A. (2021, August 22). Constant craving: How digital media turned us all into dopamine addicts. The Guardian. https://www.theguardian.com/global/2021/aug/22/how-digital-media-turned-us-all-into-dopamine-addicts-and-what-we-can-do-to-break-the-cycle

Nexus Health Systems. (2024). Excessive screen time & mental health issues. https://nexushealthsystems.com/excessive-screen-time-mental-health-issues

Newport Academy. (2022). Social media comparison and teen mental health. https://www.newportacademy.com/resources/empowering-teens/theory-of-social-comparison

Orben, A., Przybylski, A. K., Blakemore, S.-J., & Kievit, R. A. (2023). Associations between youth's daily social media use and well-being. Nature Mental Health, 1, Article 13. https://doi.org/10.1038/s44271-023-00013-0

Psychology Today. (2024). Kids and social media overload. Psychology Today. https://www.psychologytoday.com/us/blog/adolescents-explained/202408/kids-and-social-media-overload

Regehr, K. (2025, May 3). Smartphone nation. The Guardian. https://www.theguardian.com/technology/2025/may/03/digital-nutritionist-kaitlyn-regehr-parents-phone-use

Sleep Foundation. (2024). How blue light affects kids' sleep. https://www.sleepfoundation.org/children-and-sleep/how-blue-light-affects-kids-sleep

U.S. Department of Health and Human Services. (2023). Social media and youth mental health: The U.S. Surgeon General's advisory. https://www.hhs.gov/sites/default/files/sg-youth-mental-health-social-media-advisory.pdf

Yale Medicine. (2024). How social media affects your teen's mental health: A parent's guide. https://www.yalemedicine.org/news/social-media-teen-mental-health-a-parents-guide

4

Connection First — Why Attachment Still Matters in a Digital Media-Filled World

"Your presence is more powerful than any parental control app." Ambika Agarwal

Imagine this: You're sitting beside your child on the couch. You're scrolling through emails while they're watching a video. You're physically close, but emotionally, you're worlds apart.

This is the paradox of parenting in the digital age: we're often together but not connected. The presence of digital media can create physical proximity, but it often leads to emotional distance. Research shows that when using digital media, children are more likely to engage in "parallel play" each in their own digital world, rather than building the meaningful, face-to-face connections they need with their parents.

Connection is everything

For children to grow into emotionally healthy, socially aware, and resilient adults, they need one thing above all else: to feel they are seen, safe, and valued by their caregivers, no matter what the environment looks like. Secure attachment is foundational for emotional regulation, social skills, and resilience in the face of challenges. Studies consistently show that children who are securely attached tend to have better outcomes in terms of mental health, academic success, and relationships.

Screens can't replace this deep emotional bond. No matter how advanced digital media becomes, it can't replicate the power of genuine, face-to-face connection. But screens can certainly interfere with it — if we're not careful. When we allow digital media to dominate family time or distract us from being fully present, we can inadvertently create barriers to that connection. Children whose parents are frequently distracted by digital media feel less emotionally supported and more disconnected.

It all comes down to being mindful of how and when technology is being used. It's not about banning digital media entirely but about ensuring that your presence, emotionally and physically, takes precedence over the digital world. In the end, a simple conversation, a shared moment of eye contact, or playing together can do far more to nurture a child's sense of security than any parental control app could ever do.

THE SCIENCE OF ATTACHMENT

Attachment is the strong emotional link that connects a child with their primary caregiver(s). It forms in the early years of life through consistent, responsive, and warm interactions — moments when children feel safe, seen, and understood. These interactions don't need to be complex or time-consuming, but they do need to be genuine and emotionally attuned. This bond is formed through simple yet profound acts, such as:

- **Eye contact**: it's not just about looking at each other; it's about being truly present, connecting through gaze.
- **Shared smiles**: these tiny exchanges are more than just facial expressions; they communicate safety and warmth.
- **Attuned responses to needs**: responding appropriately and consistently to a child's needs helps them trust that they can rely on their caregiver.
- **Physical closeness**: hugs, cuddles, and being physically near each other provide comfort and security.
- **Meaningful conversation**: even with babies and toddlers, the act of talking, listening, and engaging in "conversations" teaches children that their thoughts and feelings matter.

This emotional bond becomes a child's internal blueprint for how relationships work, teaching them how to understand trust, safety, and connection. This bond is so powerful that it shapes how children see themselves, their caregivers, and even their social world. Research shows that children who form secure attachments tend to view the world as a place where they can take risks, learn, and explore because they feel confident that they have a safe base to return to.

Children with secure attachments are more likely to develop:

- **Stronger emotional regulation**: they can manage their feelings in healthier ways because they've experienced consistent care.
- **Better problem-solving skills**: when children feel secure, they're more willing to face challenges and think critically about solutions.
- **Higher academic achievement**: emotional security supports learning because kids feel safe to take on new tasks.
- **Healthier relationships**: secure attachment fosters healthy social skills and helps children form deeper, more empathetic connections with others.

In short, attachment lays the foundation for virtually every aspect of a child's development. When a child feels safe and valued by their caregivers, they're better equipped to navigate the world with confidence and resilience. And this attachment, while formed in the early years, continues to play a significant role as they grow older and engage with others, including the digital world.

SCREENS AND THE CONNECTION GAP

Digital media itself isn't the enemy; but distraction is.

In today's digital age, the biggest threat to attachment between parents and children isn't necessarily the device in your child's hand — it's the one in yours. As much as digital media can enhance learning, creativity, and connection, it can also create barriers to meaningful interaction when used mindlessly or without boundaries. And the effects aren't always obvious right away.

Technoference is Real

The term 'technoference' refers to the everyday interruptions in parent–child interactions caused by digital devices. Imagine visiting a local park; you might observe some parents sitting on benches, engrossed in their phones while their children play nearby, or even a parent mechanically pushing a child on a swing, their attention captured by their digital media. These are real-world examples of how digital devices can intrude on valuable moments. These disruptions occur when a parent or caregiver is distracted by their phone, tablet, or other digital device during moments when their child is seeking attention or interaction. Research shows that when caregivers are frequently preoccupied with their digital media:

- Children show more frustration and act out to regain attention. Children thrive on connection, and when they can't get their caregiver's full attention, they may use behaviors — from whining to meltdowns — to draw it back.
- Verbal and emotional exchanges drop in quality and frequency. In the middle of texting, scrolling, or checking emails, meaningful communication often slips

through the cracks. Instead of asking how their day went or sharing a moment of laughter, parents may miss an opportunity to deepen the connection.

- Kids may feel emotionally dismissed, even when parents are physically present. Research has shown that even when parents are physically next to their children, being distracted by their devices can make kids feel emotionally neglected or less important. This emotional gap can have long-term effects on attachment and emotional well-being.

And it's not just parents — when children themselves are glued to screens, the opportunity for face-to-face connection evaporates. Eye contact, open-ended conversation, and spontaneous affection are often replaced by digital content. While digital media can serve as great tools for learning and entertainment, they can also create a virtual barrier that separates children from meaningful, real-time interactions with the people around them.

The bottom line? Technology isn't inherently bad, but the secret to maintaining healthy relationships in a digital world is being mindful of how it impacts our real-life connections. Parents can work to set healthy boundaries and model balanced digital media use to ensure that digital media isn't replacing what matters most: presence, attention, and emotional availability.

STRATEGIES TO MINIMIZE TECHNOFERENCE: THE PRINCIPLES OF MINDFUL TECH USE

1. Set Digital Media-Free Zones and Times

Create specific times and spaces where technology is put away to prioritize quality interactions. For example, establish a "no devices at the dinner table" rule or make a "tech-free hour" before bed. During these times, fully engage with your child — asking about their day, playing together, or simply talking. This helps to ensure that technology doesn't interfere with key moments of connection.

2. Be Present in the Moment

Mindful digital media use is all about being present. When you're with your child, try to focus your attention solely on them, putting away devices or setting them to "Do Not Disturb." By modeling this presence, your child will learn the importance of full engagement.

3. Use Digital Media as a Tool for Connection

Rather than using digital media as a distraction, use it to connect. Watch a show together and pause it to discuss what's happening, or use digital tools to create something together, like a family photo album or a short video. This ensures that digital media becomes a shared experience that promotes interaction.

4. Schedule Digital Detox Days

Plan regular "digital detox" days or weekends where you and your family intentionally disconnect from your devices. Use this time to reconnect with nature, play board games, or engage in other activities that foster emotional bonding and face-to-face communication.

5. Create Digital Boundaries for Kids

Help your child set their own digital boundaries by encouraging breaks from digital media and balancing screen time with other activities like reading, physical play, or creative projects. Encourage them to reflect on how much time they spend on devices and whether it feels balanced with other activities.

6. Teach Emotional Availability

Show your child that emotional availability is more important than screen engagement. If your child is talking to you or seeking attention, be sure to give them your undivided attention, even if you're in the middle of something on your device.

When Disconnection Happens...

Let's face it: every parent has moments of tuning out. Maybe you were exhausted, overwhelmed, or juggling a dozen tasks at once. Perhaps you found yourself scrolling through your phone when your child needed your attention, or you lost patience when they resisted unplugging.

That's okay. The good news is that attachment is repairable. Perfection isn't the goal. What truly matters is your ability to reconnect after moments of disconnection.

Repair and Reconnection Are Key. It's easy to feel guilty about times when we aren't fully present, but research shows that the repair process is just as important for attachment as consistent, positive interactions. Children are remarkably resilient and can recover from moments of disconnection if parents try to reconnect and model emotional repair.

- Example: Saying something like, "I'm sorry I was distracted earlier. I really want to hear what you were trying to tell me", lets your child know that they are valued and that you care about making things right. Studies on emotion regulation show that children who experience both disconnection and subsequent reconnection with their caregivers are more likely to develop secure attachment styles and strong emotional resilience.

TRY THIS AT HOME: THE "EYES, EARS, HANDS" GAME

When your child is craving your attention, use this simple strategy to reconnect in a meaningful way:

Eyes – Make eye contact. This signals to your child that you're fully present and that they have your attention.

Ears – Stop talking and listen. Make sure to focus on what your child is saying without distractions.

Hands – Put your device down, even if just for a minute. Physical presence, not just verbal attention, communicates that you're truly engaged.

Just one minute of full presence can change the energy of the entire interaction, helping to rebuild trust and strengthen your emotional connection. Research on active listening and engagement shows that moments of full presence, even if brief, can significantly boost a child's sense of security and attachment. When children feel seen and heard, they are more likely to express their emotions in healthy ways.

In the Next Chapter...

In the upcoming chapter, we'll dive into setting boundaries around digital media use — but not just any boundaries. We'll focus on how to set limits that your child respects, without constant arguments or frustration. Plus, we'll explore how to build a family tech culture that reflects your unique values and goals.

References

Ainsworth, M. D. S. (1978). *Patterns of attachment: A psychological study of the strange situation*. Lawrence Erlbaum Associates.

Bowlby, J. (1988). *A secure base: Parent-child attachment and healthy human development*. Basic Books.

Cassidy, J., & Shaver, P. R. (Eds.). (2016). *Handbook of attachment: Theory, research, and clinical applications* (3rd ed.). The Guilford Press.

Gottman, J. M. (1997). *Raising an emotionally intelligent child: The heart of parenting*. Simon & Schuster.

Radesky, J. S., Kistin, C. J., Zuckerman, B., Nitzberg, K., Gross, J., Kaplan-Sanoff, M., Augustyn, M., & Silverstein, M. (2014). Patterns of mobile device use by caregivers and children during meals in fast food restaurants. *Pediatrics, 133*(4), e843–e849. https://doi.org/10.1542/peds.2013-3703

Radesky, J. S., Schumacher, J., & Zuckerman, B. (2015). Mobile and interactive media use by young children: The good, the bad, and the unknown. *Pediatrics, 135*(1), 1–3. https://doi.org/10.1542/peds.2014-2251

5

Boundaries That Stick — Rethinking Screen-Time Limits

"Boundaries aren't about control — they're about clarity, safety, and respect." Dr. Samantha Morel, PhD

How many times have you said, *"That's enough screen time,"* only to find your child ignoring you, whining, bargaining, or having a full-on meltdown?

Setting screen-time limits has become one of the most common—and exhausting parenting challenges in today's digital world. The tug-of-war over devices can feel never-ending. But here's the encouraging news: it doesn't have to be a daily battle.

What's essential isn't more control — it's more connection. When we shift from enforcing rules to fostering relationships, and from control to consistency, boundaries begin to feel less like walls and more like anchors. Children who feel understood and respected are more likely to respect boundaries.

Why a Relationship-Based Approach Works

Research consistently shows that children are more likely to accept and adhere to boundaries when they understand the *why* behind them, not because they fear consequences, but because they feel included and valued. When we explain boundaries with empathy and clarity, we're not just setting rules, we're nurturing decision-making skills.

This chapter offers a practical, developmentally informed approach to creating screen-time limits that stick. The goal is not to control your child's every move, but to cultivate a respectful, safe, and predictable environment that supports their growth.

WHY KIDS PUSH BACK ON SCREEN-TIME LIMITS

Let's face it: most digital content is engineered to be fast, fun, and incredibly hard to put down. So, it's no surprise if your child:

- Gets upset when asked to stop
- Loses track of time or struggles with transitions
- Melts down when the game or episode doesn't end naturally
- Tries to sneak in extra time or bargain for more

These reactions can feel like resistance, but they're developmentally normal. Digital platforms are designed to be addictive, with infinite scrolling, autoplay, and reward cycles that keep users engaged. Children are especially susceptible due to their still-developing self-regulation skills.

Also, consider *why* your child might be clinging to screens. Are they tired, hungry, overstimulated, or using digital media to cope with difficult feelings? These factors can heighten resistance and make transitions harder.

Importantly, pushing limits isn't necessarily disobedience, it's part of growing up. Children test boundaries not to break them, but to understand them. They're asking: *Are the rules real? Are they fair? Are you consistent?*

WHAT MAKES A BOUNDARY STICK

To reduce drama, effective boundaries need four core qualities:

1. **Clarity**: Be specific. Replace vague instructions like "a little while" with exact timeframes— "30 minutes," "2 episodes." This removes guesswork and sets clear expectations.

2. **Consistency**: Enforce the limits regularly, even when it's inconvenient. Predictability helps children feel safe and secure.

3. **Connection to Values**: Tie boundaries to what matters most to your family—whether it's time together, sleep, creativity, or physical activity. When rules reflect shared values, they carry more weight.

4. **Collaboration**: Especially with older kids, involve them in setting limits. Co-creating rules increases buy-in and shows that you respect their growing independence.

5-STEP FRAMEWORK FOR SETTING BETTER SCREEN-TIME LIMITS

Creating boundaries is not about rigid control—it's about thoughtful leadership. Here's a five-step process to set limits that work:

1. Start With Your "Why"

Before setting limits, reflect on your deeper motivations. What matters most to your family?

- Do you want more time for real-world connection?
- Are you concerned about your child's sleep, learning, or mental health?
- Are you trying to teach self-regulation for the long term?

Anchor your rules in your *values*, not a vague desire for "less screen time." The goal is intentional use of technology that supports your child's development and well-being.

2. Create a Family Tech Agreement

Make boundaries a family project. Sit down together and co-create a simple agreement that outlines:

- When screens are allowed (e.g., after school, weekends)
- Where screens are used (e.g., family room, not bedrooms)
- For how long (e.g., 30 minutes of gaming, 1 hour of TV)
- What content is encouraged (e.g., creative apps, documentaries)

Post the agreement where everyone can see it—on the fridge or near devices. Include your own commitments as a parent (e.g., "No phone during dinner") to model accountability.

3. Use Natural Stopping Points

Instead of an abrupt "20 more minutes," aim for built-in transitions:

- *"You can play until this episode ends."*
- *"When the level's done, it's time to stop."*

Pair these with gentle reminders:

- *"Five minutes until the episode ends—what will you do after?"*

This approach respects your child's engagement and makes transitions smoother.

4. Be Calm, Consistent, and Unshakable

When enforcing limit's, avoid negotiations while maintaining connection:

- **Stay grounded:** Your steady presence models emotional regulation
- **Restate with empathy:** *"I know it's tough to pause, but our 7:00 rule helps us _______"* [fill with your why: have better sleep/more family time]
- **Hold the line with warmth:** *"I'm keeping my promise to help you stick to what we agreed"*

Resist the urge to lecture or debate. A neutral, low-drama response helps de-escalate the moment and reinforces your authority.

5. Offer "Yes Spaces" After Screen Time

What comes *after* screen time matters. Transitions go better when children have something else to look forward to.

- For younger kids: Art supplies, outdoor play, music
- For teens: Snacks, conversation, alone time

These activities make screen transitions feel less like punishment and more like opportunity.

HOW TO RESPOND TO PUSHBACK

It's natural for kids to protest. Acknowledge their feelings without backing down:

- *"You're frustrated. I get it—games are fun. But the rule still stands."*

If they sneak or lie, treat it as a chance to rebuild trust—not a moral failure:

- *"We agreed on this together. When you break the rules, it affects our trust. Let's figure out how to reset."*

WHAT ABOUT WEEKENDS, TRAVEL, OR SICK DAYS?

Life happens, and routines will sometimes shift. That's okay.

- **Acknowledge the exception:** *"You're sick today, so we're relaxing the rules."*
- **Return to structure:** *"Tomorrow, we'll go back to our usual limits."*

Flexibility is part of balance. Just be intentional about returning to your baseline rhythm.

WHEN TO BE MORE HANDS-ON

Some children need firmer guidance if they:

- Are under 8 years old
- Struggle with transitions
- Use screens to avoid real-life challenges
- Show signs of difficulty with self-regulation

Teens, on the other hand, benefit more from collaboration than control. Engage them in the process so they can build the judgment needed to manage tech independently.

TRY THIS AT HOME: THE "WHEN-THEN" STRATEGY

Instead of:

> *"No video games until your chores are done."*

Try:

> *"When you finish your chores, then you can play."*

This approach is simple, consistent, and removes the power struggle. It also reinforces the idea that activities are consequential and linked, providing clear incentives for good behavior.

In the Next Chapter...

In the next chapter, we'll explore *why* digital media feels so irresistible—and what we can do about it. You'll learn:

- How persuasive tech is designed to hook attention
- Why "just one more" is so hard to resist (hint: dopamine)
- What boredom, emotion, and unmet needs have to do with screen overuse
- How to nurture *digital resilience* in your child

Because even the clearest boundaries won't matter unless your child develops the internal compass—the self-awareness, regulation, and judgment—to use technology wisely on their own.

References

Baumrind, D. (1978). Parental disciplinary patterns and social competence in children. *Youth & Society*, 9(3), 239–276. SAGE Journals.

Clifford, S., Doane, L. D., Breitenstein, R., Grimm, K. J., & Lemery-Chalfant, K. (2020). Effortful control moderates the relation between electronic-media use and objective sleep indicators in childhood. *Psychological Science*, 31(7), 822–834. SAGE Journals.

LeBourgeois, M. K., Hale, L., Chang, A. M., Akacem, L. D., Montgomery-Downs, H. E., & Buxton, O. M. (2017). Digital media and sleep in childhood and adolescence. *Pediatrics*, 140(Suppl 2), S92–S96. SAGE Journals.

Rosen, L. D., Lim, A. F., Carrier, L. M., & Cheever, N. A. (2014). An empirical examination of the educational impact of text message-induced task switching in the classroom: Educational implications and strategies to enhance learning. *Educational Psychology*, 34(5), 523–539.

Vernon, L., Barber, B. L., & Modecki, K. L. (2017). Adolescent problematic social networking and school experiences: The mediating effects of sleep disruptions and sleep quality. *Cyberpsychology, Behavior, and Social Networking*, 20(7), 430–437.

6

Digital Resilience — Helping Kids Manage Their Own Digital Media Use

"We cannot always build the future for our youth, but we can build our youth for the future." Franklin D. Roosevelt

In today's digital world, no filter, timer, or parental control app can fully shield children from what they'll eventually encounter online. The real test comes when they're alone with a screen — tired, stressed, or simply curious — and must decide for themselves:

- When to stop
- What to engage with
- How to protect their emotional and mental well-being

That's where digital resilience comes in.

What Is Digital Resilience?

Digital resilience is the ability to adapt, recover, and grow from experiences in the digital world. It's not just about protecting children from online harm — it's about equipping them with internal tools to make healthy decisions, respond thoughtfully to challenges, and thrive in a constantly evolving environment.

Kids with high digital resilience can:

- Navigate online spaces with greater self-awareness
- Manage emotional responses to digital content and interactions
- Reflect on their habits and adjust accordingly
- Make intentional choices based on their values

These skills don't just protect them online — they shape how they grow into thoughtful, confident, and responsible people.

THE CASE FOR INTERNAL STRENGTH

We can't control every corner of the internet, but we *can* raise kids who are aware, adaptable, and anchored in who they are — even in the face of algorithms designed to distract and overwhelm. Digital resilience is what empowers them to face online complexity with courage and clarity.

It's not about eliminating every risk. It's about building kids who can meet digital life with strength, skill, and self-awareness.

WHY CONTROL ISN'T ENOUGH

Many digital parenting strategies focus on external control, and they do serve a purpose. Limits like:

- Screen time boundaries
- Filters and parental controls
- Media-free zones at dinner or bedtime

...can help create structure, reduce risk, and promote healthier routines, especially for younger children.

But these tools only go so far.

Compliance ≠ Self-Regulation

If the focus is only on obedience ("because I said so"), we risk raising children who can't make thoughtful choices when we're not there to guide them. As they grow and digital access expands, they'll face situations that require:

- Independent decision-making
- Navigating peer dynamics online
- Managing stress without defaulting to a screen

Without internal regulation, they may struggle to recognize when their screen time is affecting their sleep, mood, or relationships.

WHEN CONTROL BACKFIRES

Too much monitoring or rigid enforcement can:

- Lead to sneaky behavior or secrecy
- Spark power struggles
- Prevent kids from understanding *why* they're drawn to their devices

Overly controlling parenting can reduce kids' sense of autonomy and emotional regulation, both essential for building digital resilience.

THE BETTER GOAL: INTERNAL CONTROL

Instead of asking, *"How do I stop my child from using digital media?"*, try asking:

"How do I help my child understand and manage their own use of digital media?"

That shift — from control to coaching — is important for long-term digital well-being. External limits are important. But internal skills are what last.

The 3 Core Skills of Digital Resilience

Digital resilience doesn't just "happen." It's built through guided reflection, supportive conversations, and everyday practice. These three skills are foundational:

1. SELF-AWARENESS

The first step is helping kids tune into how digital media affects them physically, emotionally, and mentally.

Ask open-ended, non-judgmental questions like:

- *"How do you feel after playing that game?"*
- *"Did that video make you feel more relaxed or more irritated?"*
- *"What's your body telling you right now?"*

These questions build interoception — the ability to sense and interpret internal signals like tension, restlessness, or calm. This awareness lays the foundation for emotional intelligence and decision-making.

Over time, kids learn to notice:

- When they're overstimulated or emotionally drained
- Which content uplifts versus depletes them
- When their bodies need a break

Encouraging this kind of reflection helps children develop habits that support and not sabotage their well-being.

2. SELF-REGULATION

Self-regulation means managing impulses and emotions, especially when faced with endless scroll, autoplay videos, or emotionally charged content.

Support your child's regulation skills by:

- Using timers as check-in points rather than cutoffs
- Encouraging stretch or water breaks
- Modeling mindful behavior: *"I'm feeling overwhelmed, so I'm going to take a screen break."*
- Inviting older kids to set their own use goals — and reflect on how those goals feel over time

These small habits strengthen their mental brakes, supporting not just healthy tech use, but also future decision-making in friendships, school, and life.

3. VALUES-BASED DECISION-MAKING

As kids grow, they begin shaping their digital identities. Help them make choices that align with who they are and what they care about.

Try saying:

- *"You're so creative — how can you use your screen time to make something?"*
- *"That video left you feeling down — what kind of content lifts you up instead?"*
- *"Kindness matters to you. How can you show that in your online interactions?"*

This approach taps into intrinsic motivation — where choices come from values, not pressure. It nurtures integrity, ownership, and purpose in their digital lives.

Why Kids Turn to Screens in the First Place

It's important to understand that kids (and adults) often turn to digital media to regulate their emotions. Not because they're lazy or addicted — but because screens offer fast, easy relief.

COMMON EMOTION-DRIVEN TRIGGERS:

- **Boredom**: Instant stimulation feels easier than inventing something to do
- **Loneliness**: Social media simulates connection, even if it's shallow
- **Stress or anxiety**: Games or videos distract from discomfort
- **Frustration**: Scrolling or zoning out offers a sense of control
- **Avoidance**: Screens help dodge hard or uncomfortable tasks

Helping children *name and understand* these feelings gives them the power to choose differently.

HOW TO BUILD EMOTIONAL LITERACY

Try saying:

- *"I noticed you picked up your device after that hard math assignment. Are you feeling a little frustrated?"*
- *"Sometimes we reach for a screen when something feels off. Is there another way you might want to feel better right now?"*

These conversations teach kids to pause, reflect, and eventually choose healthier ways to manage their emotions.

Healthy Alternatives to Digital Coping

Offer screen-free strategies that support expression, connection, and movement:

- Drawing, journaling, or crafting
- Playing outside or getting active
- Talking with a trusted friend or adult
- Listening to music
- Taking quiet time or practicing mindfulness

The goal isn't to ban digital media — it's to help children recognize when it serves them, and when it doesn't.

Celebrate the Wins

Often, we focus on digital mistakes. But recognizing positive choices is just as, if not more, important.

Here's what to look for:

- **Turning off a device without being reminded**: *"I noticed you stopped when the timer rang — that shows real responsibility."*
- **Taking a break to reset**: *"You stepped away when that chat got stressful —that's mature self-awareness."*
- **Using tech creatively**: *"You really made something meaningful with that app — I love how you brought your ideas to life."*
- **Setting healthy boundaries**: *"Turning off those notifications shows you're in charge of your time — nice job."*

In the Next Chapter...

We'll dive into the world of social media and self-image, exploring how online platforms affect how kids see themselves, compare themselves, and find connections and how you can protect their self-worth in the process.

Because raising healthy digital kids means teaching them not just *how to manage digital media*, but how to stay grounded in who they are, on-screen and off.

References

American Academy of Pediatrics. (2011). The Impact of Social Media on Children, Adolescents, and Families. *Pediatrics*, 127(4), 800–804. https://doi.org/10.1542/peds.2011-0054Pediatrics

Craig, A. D. (2002). How do you feel? Interoception: the sense of the physiological condition of the body. *Nature Reviews Neuroscience*, 3(8), 655–666. https://doi.org/10.1038/nrn894

Deci, E. L., & Ryan, R. M. (2000). The "what" and "why" of goal pursuits: Human needs and the self-determination of behavior. *Psychological Inquiry*, 11(4), 227–268. https://doi.org/10.1207/S15327965PLI1104_01

Denham, S. A., Bassett, H. H., & Wyatt, T. (2012). The socialization of emotional competence. In P. K. Smith & C. H. Hart (Eds.), *The Wiley-Blackwell Handbook of Childhood Social Development* (2nd ed., pp. 413–433). Wiley-Blackwell.

Füstös, J., Gramann, K., Herbert, B. M., & Pollatos, O. (2013). On the embodiment of emotion regulation: Interoceptive awareness facilitates reappraisal. *Social Cognitive and Affective Neuroscience*, 8(8), 911–917. https://doi.org/10.1093/scan/nss089

Hinduja, S., & Patchin, J. W. (2017). Cultivating youth resilience to prevent bullying and cyberbullying victimization. *Child Abuse & Neglect*, 73, 51–62. https://doi.org/10.1016/j.chiabu.2017.09.010 Cyberbullying Research Center.

Livingstone, S., & Byrne, J. (2018). Parenting in the digital age: The challenges of parental responsibility in comparative perspective. In G. Mascheroni, C. Ponte, & A. Jorge (Eds.), *Digital Parenting: The Challenges for Families in the Digital Age* (pp. 19–30). Nordicom.

Livingstone, S., & Helsper, E. J. (2008). Parental mediation of children's internet use. *Journal of Broadcasting & Electronic Media*, 52(4), 581–599. https://doi.org/10.1080/08838150802437396

Odgers, C. L., & Jensen, M. R. (2020). Annual Research Review: Adolescent mental health in the digital age: Facts, fears, and future directions. *Journal of Child Psychology and Psychiatry*, 61(3), 336–348. https://doi.org/10.1111/jcpp.13190

Soenens, B., & Vansteenkiste, M. (2010). A theoretical upgrade of the concept of parental psychological control: Proposing new insights on the basis of self-determination theory. *Developmental Review*, 30(1), 74–99. https://doi.org/10.1016/j.dr.2009.11.001

Tynes, B. M., Rose, C. A., & Williams, D. R. (2015). The development and validation of the Online Victimization Scale for adolescents. *Cyberpsychology: Journal of Psychosocial Research on Cyberspace*, 9(2), Article 2. https://doi.org/10.5817/CP2015-2-2

Twenge, J. M., & Campbell, W. K. (2018). Associations between screen time and lower psychological well-being among children and adolescents: Evidence from a population-based study. *Preventive Medicine Reports*, 12, 271–283. https://doi.org/10.1016/j.pmedr.2018.10.003

Valkenburg, P. M., & Piotrowski, J. T. (2017). Plugged In: How Media Attract and Affect Youth. Yale University Press.

Zhou, Q., Chen, S. H., & Main, A. (2012). Commonalities and differences in the research on children's effortful control and executive function: A call for an integrated model of self-regulation. *Child Development Perspectives*, 6(2), 112–121. https://doi.org/10.1111/j.1750-8606.2011.00176.x

7

Likes, Looks, and the Mirror Effect — Self-Image in the Age of Social Media

"When kids see themselves through filters, our job is to help them see their worth more clearly." Wendy Toth

Once upon a time, kids figured out who they were through scraped knees in the backyard, awkward first crushes, school projects that went sideways, and words of encouragement (or redirection) from adults who cared. It was messy, slow, and often confusing — but it was real.

Today, many children are growing up with a different kind of mirror. It's always on, always comparing, always reacting. That mirror is social media — and it's changing how kids see themselves.

The Hidden Curriculum of Social Media

Apps like Instagram, TikTok, and Snapchat aren't just digital playgrounds — they're powerful classrooms. And even though there's no official syllabus, kids are learning a lot.

Without saying a word, social media teaches what kind of beauty gets rewarded, what success *looks* like (even if it's not real), and how fast you're supposed to respond to avoid being left out. It sends subtle, persistent messages that shape how kids think about their value, especially during adolescence, a time when the brain becomes extra sensitive to social feedback, driven to compare, and hungry to figure out who it's becoming.

Even when kids know that what they're seeing is filtered or curated, it still affects them. A teen might scroll through a friend's vacation post and wonder, *"Why doesn't my life feel like that?"* Or they might spend 20 minutes adjusting a selfie, finally posting it, only to delete it when the likes don't roll in fast enough.

This is what psychologists sometimes call the Mirror Effect. Social media becomes a kind of funhouse mirror — reflecting not who kids are, but a distorted, edited version of life that they can start to believe is the norm.

WHEN THE MIRROR WARPS THE REFLECTION

Kids who spend hours a day on social media — sometimes without even meaning to — may start to see themselves through that warped lens. And it affects more than just body image.

Some kids begin to judge their worth by likes and follower counts. Others feel deflated when they compare their lives to others' highlight reels. Seeing friends together without them can spark real feelings of exclusion. And even when they know it's all curated, the sting is real.

Research echoes this loud and clear. A 2022 Common Sense Media report found that over one-third of teens said social media made them feel worse about their bodies. The American Psychological Association links heavy social media use with increased anxiety, depression, and low self-esteem, especially in girls.

Part of the reason? The adolescent brain is wired for reward. Each like, comment, or tag triggers a burst of dopamine — the brain's feel-good chemical. But unlike a slice of cake or a high-five, social media offers no natural stopping point. The feedback loop is endless. And for a developing mind, that can be overwhelming.

What Parents Can Do: Rebalancing the Mirror

We can't throw out the mirror altogether — and honestly, we don't need to. Social media isn't all bad. But we *can* help kids adjust their focus. That means teaching them to reflect more clearly, trust what they see within, and define their worth on deeper terms than likes and filters.

Here's how:

Make Conversations About Image a Habit, not a Lecture

Don't wait for a crisis or a viral story to open the conversation. Weave small, open-ended questions into everyday moments — on a walk, in the car, or during dinner:

- *"Have you ever seen something online that made you feel left out?"*
- *"What do you think about those filters people use in selfies?"*
- *"Who on your feed makes you feel better about yourself?"*

These kinds of questions don't just spark reflection — they build trust. They say, *this is a safe place to talk about stuff that's hard to name.*

Teach Media Literacy Like You'd Teach Driving

No one hands over car keys without practice and supervision. Social media should be no different. Help your child decode what they're seeing:

- *"That influencer is likely being paid — their job is to sell, not to tell the whole truth."*
- *"That video probably took 15 tries. It's not as effortless as it looks."*
- *"Remember — most people only post the best 5% of their lives."*

This isn't about scaring kids away from the internet. It's about giving them tools to see through the sparkle — and to ask better questions about what they're absorbing.

Encourage Creation Over Comparison

Scrolling passively can leave kids feeling small and behind. But using digital platforms to *create* — to share their voice, humor, interests, or talents — builds confidence and purpose.

Invite them to:

- Post something they made that they're proud of
- Share thoughts or causes that matter to them
- Use stories or reels to reflect real life, not just filtered moments

When kids use social media to express rather than impress, their experience shifts from comparison to creativity.

Model Body Neutrality and Healthy Tech Habits

Kids pay closer attention to our actions than our words. So be intentional about how you talk about your body, your tech use, and your self-worth.

Try saying things like:

- *"I'm grateful for what my body lets me do today."*
- *"I need a break from scrolling — I want some space to just live in the moment."*
- *"That photo wasn't flattering, but hey — I was having fun, and that's what matters."*

These small choices add up. When kids see you prioritizing rest over endless scrolling or choosing self-compassion over criticism, it permits them to do the same.

TRY THIS AT HOME: THE "DIGITAL MIRRORS" CHECK-IN

Once a month — maybe over Sunday pancakes or during a walk — do a gentle family digital check-in. You don't need a worksheet or a timer. Just a few real questions:

- *"What's one thing online that made you feel good about yourself this week?"*
- *"Did anything you saw make you feel less than, or unsure about yourself?"*
- *"Is there anything in your feed you want to see more of?"*
- *"Anyone or anything you might want to mute for a while?"*

This isn't about micromanaging your child's feed. It's about reminding them — and yourself — that we *can* shape what we take in. We can clean the mirror a little.

KNOW THE RED FLAGS

Sometimes the mirror needs more than cleaning — it needs recalibration. Watch for signs that social media is taking a toll:

- Obsession with likes or followers
- Withdrawing from real-life friends or activities

- Mood crashes after screen time
- Frequent negative self-talk or body complaints
- Hiding or sneaking screen use

If you see these signs, don't panic. Open a door, not a lecture. A simple, "Hey, I noticed you seemed a little down after being online — want to talk about it?" can go a long way.

Final Thoughts: Helping Them See What's Real

We can't fully control the digital world our kids live in. But we *can* guide how they navigate it — and how they see themselves through it.

We can remind them that their worth isn't found in filters or follows. That their bodies don't need fixing. That the version of themselves they post isn't nearly as important as the one they're becoming — slowly, awkwardly, and beautifully — offline.

Social media might be the mirror they look into. But with your help, they'll learn to reflect on what truly matters.

In the Next Chapter...

We'll look at family culture and digital media use — how to create a shared set of values, rituals, and routines that shape the digital habits in your home, without constant battles or power struggles.

Because your home environment sets the stage for how kids feel, connect, and grow — on-screen and off.

References

American Psychological Association. (2023, May 9). *Teens are stuck on their screens. Here's how to protect them*. TIME. https://time.com/7177874/teen-video-viewing-guidance-apa/

Center for the Developing Adolescent. (2023). *Social media and adolescents, part 1: "We have the entire world in our back pockets"*. https://developingadolescent.semel.ucla.edu/steps-for-youth/item/social-media-and-adolescents-part-1

De, D., El Jamal, M., Aydemir, E., & Khera, A. (2025). Social media algorithms and teen addiction: Neurophysiological impact and ethical considerations. *Cureus, 17*(1), e77145. https://doi.org/10.7759/cureus.77145

Doheny, K., & Lighthall, N. (2023). Neural reactivity to social reward moderates the association between social media use and momentary positive affect in adolescents. *Affective Science*. https://doi.org/10.1007/s42761-024-00237-1

Medical Daily. (2016, May 31). *The teenage brain on social media: Facebook and Instagram 'likes' trigger same reward system as eating chocolate*. https://www.medicaldaily.com/teenage-brain-social-media-facebook-instagram-likes-eating-chocolate-388333

Sherman, L. E., Payton, A. A., Hernandez, L. M., Greenfield, P. M., & Dapretto, M. (2016). The power of the like in adolescence: Effects of peer influence on neural and behavioral responses to social media. *Psychological Science, 27*(7), 1027–1035. https://doi.org/10.1177/0956797616645673

Telzer, E. H. (2023). *Adolescent brain development and social media use*. Children and Screens. https://www.childrenandscreens.org/learn-explore/research/adolescent-brain-development-and-social-media-use-eva-telzer-phd/

Time Staff. (2024, June 17). *Why the U.S. Surgeon General wants a warning label for social media*. TIME. https://time.com/6989369/us-surgeon-general-warning-label-social-media/

Verywell Health. (2020, April 7). *What is dopamine?* https://www.verywellhealth.com/dopamine-5086831

Wired Staff. (2016, May 31). *What social media does to a teenager's brain*. Wired. https://www.wired.com/story/what-happens-to-teenage-brain-on-social-media/

8

Digital Media in the Family System — Creating a Healthy Digital Culture at Home

"It's not just about what your kids do online. It's about how your family lives with technology together." Milovidov

When we think about screen time, we often zoom in on the individual, usually the child. How much time are *they* spending online? What content are *they* consuming? But digital media doesn't exist in a vacuum; it is an integral part of a larger system, and that system is your family.

From the moment someone pulls out a phone at dinner to how bedtime routines unfold, technology subtly weaves itself into the everyday rhythm of home life. It's not inherently good or bad — but how you choose to manage it *together* makes all the difference.

This chapter isn't about creating a tech-free household or battling screens like the enemy. It's about building a *conscious, connected digital culture* — one where digital media supports your family's values instead of eroding them.

Your Family Already Has a Digital Culture — Whether You Meant to Create One or Not

Every family has unwritten rules, habits, and digital media rhythms. The question is:

- Are they intentional?
- Have they grown out of convenience?
- Is it okay to scroll during meals?
- Are phones allowed in bedrooms?
- What happens when screen time ends — conflict or calm?
- How do we spend time together *without* devices?

If you don't shape your family's digital culture on purpose, it tends to shape itself — often around whatever feels easiest in the moment. Over time, that can create confusion for kids, increase tension, and diminish connection.

DIGITAL MEDIA IS PART OF THE SYSTEM

Think of digital media not as isolated tools, but as part of a family ecosystem. What one person does with digital media impacts the whole system:

- A parent scrolling during story time
- A teen texting through dinner
- A child melting down after abrupt screen time limits

These moments aren't failures — they're signals. Opportunities to reflect, reset, and realign how digital media is functioning in your home.

THE POWER OF EXPLICIT FAMILY AGREEMENTS

Instead of relying on individual rules or constant corrections, consider creating clear, shared family agreements around digital media use. These are not punishments — they're collaborative boundaries built around your values and connection.

Host a Family Meeting About Digital Media

Bring everyone together — not to lecture, but to listen. Create space for honest conversation.

Ask:

- What do we love about our devices?
- What do we not love — what gets in the way?
- What kind of family time do we want more of?
- How can we use digital media in a way that supports our goals?

Let kids (even young ones) contribute. When children have a say, they're more invested in the outcome.

Co-Create a Family Tech Agreement

Decide together on 3–5 core agreements that reflect your family values. Examples might include:

- No phones during meals
- Devices sleep in the kitchen overnight
- Screen-free Saturdays until noon
- Ask before downloading new apps
- Be as kind online as we are in real life

Post the agreement somewhere visible — not as strict rules, but as shared commitments to a healthy digital culture.

Review and Adjust Regularly

As kids grow, habits evolve. Revisit your family agreement regularly and reflect:

- What's working well?
- What feels hard or outdated?
- What new digital media challenges have emerged?

Keep it flexible and responsive to your family's changing needs.

CREATING DIGITAL MEDIA-FREE RITUALS THAT STRENGTHEN CONNECTION

Rituals are the heartbeat of family culture — and digital media-free rituals help anchor us in presence, joy, and togetherness. These don't have to be elaborate. A few simple, consistent moments go a long way.

Ideas to try:

- Tech-free dinners (start with one per week)
- Sunday unplugged mornings
- Evening walks or puzzles together
- Family movie night — with phones parked elsewhere
- Creative time (drawing, music, writing) with devices set aside

These aren't about rejecting technology. They're about making room for what really matters.

MODELING MATTERS — MORE THAN YOU THINK

Children are always watching. The way *you* interact with technology teaches them how to relate to it.

- Do you put your phone away when they talk to you?
- Do you reach for your device when stressed — or for support?
- Do you take breaks from digital media yourself?

You don't have to be perfect. But small, consistent actions — like saying, *"I'm putting my phone down so I can really listen"* — send powerful messages about presence and priority.

TRY THIS AT HOME: MONTHLY FAMILY TECH REFLECTION

Carve out a regular time — maybe over dinner or during a walk — to reflect on your family's digital habits together. Keep it light and connection-focused, not critical.

Sample questions:

- What's one thing you enjoyed online this week?
- Was anything online stressful or upsetting?
- What's one way we could have more fun offline together?
- Are there any digital media habits we want to shift?

Let this be a moment of curiosity, growth, and togetherness, not correction.

Screens Can Support — or Strain — Mental Health

Remember: digital media isn't the enemy, but it can have a powerful influence. Notifications, social comparison, dopamine-driven apps, and disrupted sleep can all impact your child's emotional well-being — and your own.

By treating digital media as a family issue, not just an individual challenge, you shift from managing to *meaning making*. You move from control to connection.

Together, you can create a home where technology fits around your family's values not the other way around.

In the Next Chapter...

We'll dive into the challenges of overuse, addiction, and problem habits — what's normal, what's worrisome, and how to respond with skill and compassion when digital media use starts getting in the way of life.

Because all families face challenges, what matters most is how we respond — together.

References

Common Sense Media. (2020). *The Common Sense census: Media use by tweens and teens, 2020*. https://www.commonsensemedia.org/research

Coyne, S. M., Padilla-Walker, L. M., & Howard, E. (2013). Emerging in a digital world: A decade review of media use, effects, and gratifications in emerging adulthood. *Emerging Adulthood, 1*(2), 125–137. https://doi.org/10.1177/2167696813479782

Hiniker, A., Schoenebeck, S., & Kientz, J. A. (2016). Not at the dinner table: Parents' and children's perspectives on family technology rules. *Proceedings of the 19th ACM Conference on Computer-Supported Cooperative Work & Social Computing*, 1376–1389. https://doi.org/10.1145/2818048.2819940

Livingstone, S., & Blum-Ross, A. (2020). *Parenting for a digital future: How hopes and fears about technology shape children's lives*. Oxford University Press.

Radesky, J. S., & Christakis, D. A. (2016). Increased screen time: Implications for early childhood development and behavior. *Pediatric Clinics, 63*(5), 827–839. https://doi.org/10.1016/j.pcl.2016.06.006

Rideout, V., & Robb, M. B. (2019). *The Common Sense census: Inside the 21st-century classroom*. Common Sense Media. https://www.commonsensemedia.org/research

Steiner-Adair, C., & Barker, T. (2013). *The big disconnect: Protecting childhood and family relationships in the digital age*. Harper.

9

When It Becomes Too Much — Understanding and Responding to Problematic Digital Media Use

"Screen time isn't inherently bad — but when it takes over, it's time to pause and reflect." Dr. Michael Rich

For some children (and adults), digital media use can move from helpful to harmful. When digital engagement begins to interfere with daily functioning — like school, sleep, relationships, or mood — it's time to take a closer look.

What Is Problematic Digital Media Use?

Researchers describe *problematic use* as digital behaviors that:

- Interfere with basic needs (like sleep or exercise)
- Cause emotional distress (e.g., anxiety, irritability)

- Disrupt social and academic functioning
- Become compulsive, even when negative consequences occur

WARNING SIGNS OF OVERUSE

- **Escalating Time Online**: Gradual increases in digital media use can become chronic without awareness. Monitoring tools or screen-time use reports can help families track trends.
- **Difficulty Disconnecting**: If your child resists logging off or shows distress when devices are taken away, this may indicate emotional reliance on digital content.
- **School Struggles**: Declining grades, procrastination, or poor concentration may reflect excessive digital distractions.
- **Emotional Disruption**: Digital media use that correlates with mood swings, irritability, or sadness may be displacing emotional regulation.
- **Social Withdrawal**: If your child is increasingly avoiding face-to-face interaction, it may signal digital media-related avoidance.
- **Sleep Disruption**: Digital media use at bedtime suppresses melatonin, making it harder to fall asleep and stay asleep, with lasting effects on mood, memory, and behavior.

WHY OVERUSE IS A CONCERN

- **Dopamine and Digital Design**: Digital platforms are designed to be addictive — using algorithms, variable rewards, and "likes" to create dopamine feedback loops. This makes self-control hard, especially for developing brains.

- **Developmental Imbalance**: Children need practice managing boredom, conflict, and emotion offline. When screens replace those experiences, emotional development may be delayed.
- **Interrupted Sleep**: Insufficient sleep affects everything from focus to emotional regulation to physical growth. Kids using digital media late into the evening may be sleep-deprived — and not even realize it.

HOW TO RESPOND: APPROACHING THE SITUATION WITH COMPASSION AND CLARITY

Helping your child manage digital media use isn't about control—it's about connection. Kids need guidance, not punishment, and when we respond with empathy and structure, we support healthier habits that can last a lifetime.

Start with Understanding, Not Punishment

When digital media use starts to feel out of control, your first instinct might be to restrict it immediately. But starting with curiosity opens the door to real change.

Try starting a conversation like:

- *"Looks like you've been spending more time on your phone lately. What's been drawing you in?"*
- *"I can tell it's hard to turn off the game. Want to talk about what makes that tough?"*

These types of questions show your child that you're not out to punish them, you're trying to understand their experience. This builds trust and invites honesty.

Why this matters: Children and teens often turn to screens for emotional regulation when they're feeling lonely, overwhelmed, or anxious. Understanding what they're using screens *for* can help you better address the root cause of overuse.

Set Limits Collaboratively

Rather than laying down hard rules, work together to create balanced guidelines. When children are involved in setting boundaries, they're more likely to follow them.

Steps you can take together:

- Agree on daily or weekly screen time limits (outside of school/work)
- Prioritize homework, chores, sleep, and meals before recreational digital media use
- Let your child decide how and when to use their screen time—for example, choosing between gaming, chatting with friends, or watching videos

What the research says: Autonomy-supportive parenting—where children have a voice in decision-making—is linked to greater motivation, emotional regulation, and healthy behavior patterns. When kids feel heard, they're more likely to listen.

Teach Self-Awareness

Kids (and adults!) often use digital media without realizing how it affects their mood, energy, or focus. Helping your child reflect on their habits builds lifelong self-regulation skills.

Ask reflective questions like:

- *"How do you usually feel before you go online? How do you feel after?"*
- *"What happens to your mood or focus when you've been using your phone too much?"*
- *"What helps you take a break or log off when you need to?"*

You can use screen time tracking apps or a simple screen journal to help them build awareness. Even a weekly check-in can highlight patterns they hadn't noticed.

Tip: Learning to recognize their own "red flags"—like headaches, crankiness, or zoning out—can empower your child to make healthier choices on their own.

Promote Offline Joy

It's easier to say "less screen time" when there's something enjoyable to say "yes" to. Instead of focusing on what your child is giving up, help them rediscover the fun and satisfaction of offline life.

Great alternatives might include:

- Physical activities: sports, biking, walking, dancing
- Creative outlets: art, writing, music, building
- Social connections: inviting a friend over, joining a club
- Family time: game night, cooking together, outings

The goal isn't to remove digital media entirely—it's to re-balance your child's time so they're also engaging in real-world experiences that support healthy development.

Fun fact: Engaging in meaningful offline activities has been linked to higher self-esteem and life satisfaction in teens, even more than how much screen time they have.

Protect Sleep

Sleep is one of the first casualties of too much digital media use, especially in the evening. Blue light from screens interferes with the body's melatonin production, making it harder to fall and stay asleep.

Tips for better sleep hygiene:

- Set a consistent "screens-off" rule at least 60 minutes before bed
- Create relaxing bedtime routines: reading, drawing, stretching, or listening to music

- Remove phones and tablets from the bedroom or keep them in airplane mode overnight

Why it matters: Children and teens need 8–10 hours of sleep per night for emotional regulation, memory, and learning. Chronic sleep deprivation from late-night scrolling can lead to irritability, lower academic performance, and even depressive symptoms.

SEEK HELP IF NEEDED

If you're seeing signs of anxiety, depression, or significant behavior change, consider working with a mental health professional. Cognitive-behavioral therapy (CBT) and family counseling can be effective in treating digital overuse and emotional health concerns.

In the Next Chapter...

We'll explore the future of technology — how to prepare your child for a world where digital media is an inescapable part of life, and how to equip them with the tools they need to navigate it safely, healthily, and responsibly.

Because technology isn't going anywhere, with the right skills and mindset, your child can grow up to be a mindful, balanced user — one who can use technology to thrive, not just survive.

References

Domoff, S. E., Harrison, K., Gearhardt, A. N., Gentile, D. A., Lumeng, J. C., & Miller, A. L. (2017). Development and validation of the Problematic Media Use Measure: A parent-report measure of screen media "addiction" in children. Psychology of Popular Media Culture, 8(1), 2–11. https://doi.org/10.1037/ppm0000163

Kardefelt-Winther, D. (2014). A conceptual and methodological critique of internet addiction research: Towards a model of compensatory internet use. Computers in Human Behavior, 31, 351–354. https://doi.org/10.1016/j.chb.2013.10.059

Kuss, D. J., & Griffiths, M. D. (2015). Social networking sites and addiction: Ten lessons learned. International Journal of Environmental Research and Public Health, 12(3), 1286–1306. https://doi.org/10.3390/ijerph120201286

Leone, M. J., & Sigman, M. (2020). Effects of late-night mobile phone use on sleep and academic performance: A longitudinal study in adolescents. Journal of Adolescence, 84, 173–181. https://doi.org/10.1016/j.adolescence.2020.08.004

Soenens, B., & Vansteenkiste, M. (2010). A theoretical upgrade of the concept of parental psychological control: Proposing new insights on the basis of self-determination theory. Developmental Review, 30(1), 74–99. https://doi.org/10.1016/j.dr.2009.11.001

Twenge, J. M., & Campbell, W. K. (2018). Associations between screen time and lower psychological well-being among children and adolescents: Evidence from a population-based study. ("Associations between screen time ... preview & related info - Mendeley") Preventive Medicine Reports, 12, 271–283. https://doi.org/10.1016/j.pmedr.2018.10.003

10

Preparing for the Digital Future — Equipping Your Child for Lifelong Success in a Tech-Driven World

"The future is already here — it's just not evenly distributed" William Gibson

We live in an era where technology isn't just a tool — it's a way of life. From artificial intelligence to virtual reality, digital advances are reshaping every aspect of our society: how we work, how we learn, and even how we relate to each other.

For your child, the digital future is already unfolding, and it's more than just the next cool app or game. It's the world they'll inherit — a world that demands a different set of skills than those required by previous generations. The question is: How do you prepare them for it?

In this chapter, we'll explore how to equip your child with the tools and mindset they need to thrive in this rapidly evolving digital landscape.

The Need for Digital Literacy — It's More Than Just Tech Skills

In the past, we focused largely on academic and social skills to prepare kids for success. Today, however, digital literacy has become just as important.

But digital literacy isn't just about knowing how to use a smartphone or the latest software. It's about navigating the digital world with competence, curiosity, and critical thinking. It's about understanding how digital media impacts their lives, their relationships, and future opportunities.

WHAT DOES DIGITAL LITERACY LOOK LIKE?

Digital literacy includes several key components:

1. **Technical Skills**: These are the basic abilities required to use various devices and platforms, like smartphones, computers, and apps. However, as technology evolves rapidly, this will become even more of a foundational skill that must be built upon.

2. **Critical Thinking and Problem Solving**: Your child needs to be able to critically evaluate digital information. This means questioning sources, recognizing bias, and differentiating fact from fiction in an increasingly complex online world.

3. **Digital Safety and Ethics**: Teaching your child how to protect their privacy, be mindful of digital footprints, and behave ethically online is essential. They need to understand the importance of maintaining personal boundaries and respecting others' privacy.

4. **Digital Citizenship**: This is about teaching your child to be a responsible and respectful participant in digital spaces. It's about fostering kindness, empathy, and cooperation — both online and offline.

5. **Emotional Resilience**: It's important to help your child develop emotional resilience in the face of digital pressures, whether it's cyberbullying, digital comparisons, or the constant flood of information.

PRACTICAL STEPS FOR BUILDING DIGITAL LITERACY

Start Early, Start Simple

Digital literacy doesn't need to wait until middle school or high school. Start introducing concepts early, even with young children. Teach them the basics of safe digital media use, such as understanding why certain websites are off-limits or how to keep personal information private. For example, when browsing the web together, you can say:

- *"We don't click on links we don't recognize, because some websites can be dangerous."*
- *"Let's make sure we never share your name, address, or school online."*
- *"If you see a pop-up asking for your personal information, what should we do? Right, we don't give that information out."*

Model Critical Thinking

Encourage your child to think critically about the media they consume. Watch shows, read articles, or play games together, and discuss what they see. Ask questions like:

- *"What point do you think the author is making?"*
- *"How do you know this information is trustworthy?"*
- *"What is the impact of this on people's emotions or opinions?"* For example, after watching a commercial for a toy, you can ask, *"What do you think the commercial wants us to believe about this toy?"* This helps your child learn to approach digital content with curiosity and skepticism, developing an understanding of media bias and the persuasive nature of advertising.
- *"How can we tell if this website is giving us good information?"* This helps your child practice evaluating online content for truthfulness and credibility.

Encourage Creative Digital Expression

As your child gets older, provide opportunities for them to create, not just consume, digital media. Whether it's building a website, creating videos, writing a blog, or coding an app, creative digital expression can enhance critical thinking and problem-solving skills. For example, you could say:

- *"Why don't you create a video about your favorite hobby and share it with the family? What message would you like to communicate?"*
- *"Let's design a website about something you care about. How can we organize it to make it fun and informative?"*

Teach Digital Ethics

Discuss concepts of digital ethics, like respecting others online, understanding the consequences of sharing personal information, and being kind in digital communication. Help your child understand the importance of being a good digital citizen and how actions online can have real-life consequences. For instance, you can ask questions like:

- *"How would you feel if someone said something hurtful to you online?"*
- *"If we share a photo of our family, who else could see it?"*
- *" How can we help if we see someone being bullied on the internet?"*

Set Guidelines for Healthy Tech Use

As your child grows more independent, it's important to involve them in creating tech use guidelines. These should include rules about privacy, boundaries, and balance, and should evolve as your child grows and takes on more responsibility. For example, when setting up rules together, you could ask:

- *"How much screen time do you think is okay each day?"*
- *"What should we do if you feel like you've spent too much time on your device?"*

- *"How can we make sure that tech doesn't get in the way of your sleep, homework, or outdoor play?"*

Emotional Resilience in a Digital World

One of the biggest challenges your child will face is learning to manage the emotional impact of being constantly connected. Social media, digital comparisons, and the endless flow of content can take a toll on a child's mental health if not managed properly.

Here's how to help your child build emotional resilience in a digital world:

Promote Healthy Social Media Habits

Encourage your child to be mindful of how social media makes them feel. Talk about the "highlight reel" effect — how people often post only their best moments, which can create unrealistic expectations. Help them understand that real life isn't curated, and that authenticity is more valuable than comparisons.

Teach Them to Set Boundaries

Help your child develop the ability to say no to digital distractions. Whether it's turning off notifications or taking digital breaks, boundaries help prevent overwhelm and foster a sense of control.

Encourage Face-to-Face Interactions

Nothing beats in-person connections when it comes to building emotional resilience. Encourage your child to spend time with friends and family offline — to build relationships in the real world rather than relying on digital interactions.

Promote Mindfulness and Digital Detox

Teach your child mindfulness techniques, such as deep breathing or journaling, to help them manage stress. Encourage regular digital detoxes, where the family takes breaks from screens to focus on relaxation, outdoor activities, and real-world connections.

The Role of Parents in Shaping the Digital Future

As parents, it's easy to feel overwhelmed by the sheer scale of digital changes. But your role as a guide has never been more important. You can steer the ship toward positive, meaningful engagement with technology.

Here's how to continue supporting your child in this digital world:

Be Informed

Stay up to date on the latest digital trends, apps, and platforms. Educate yourself about emerging technologies like artificial intelligence, virtual reality, and gaming, so you can help your child navigate these tools with awareness.

Stay Engaged

Keep the conversation about technology ongoing. Ask your child about their online experiences, who they're interacting with, and what they're learning. Stay curious about their digital world and be a resource for questions.

Foster Open Communication

Maintain an open-door policy when it comes to discussing online experiences. Be a safe space for your child to share their concerns, whether it's a troubling conversation with a friend online or a game that's becoming too addictive.

In the Next Chapter...

The final chapter will summarize some of the key principles of raising a healthy child in a digital world and provide practical tips for maintaining balance and harmony as technology continues to evolve.

Because, while digital media use will continue to shape our future, we have the power to ensure that our children grow into capable, balanced individuals — ready to navigate and thrive in the digital world ahead.

References

Blum-Ross, A., & Livingstone, S. (2016). From youth voice to young entrepreneurs: The individualization of digital media and learning. Journal of Digital and Media Literacy, 4(1), 1–16.

Goleman, D., & Davidson, R. J. (2017). Altered traits: Science reveals how meditation changes your mind, brain, and body. Avery.

Kahne, J., & Bowyer, B. (2017). Educating for democracy in a digital age: Media literacy education's role in the era of fake news. Peabody Journal of Education, 92(1), 23–35. https://doi.org/10.1080/0161956X.2016.1265347

Livingstone, S., & Helsper, E. J. (2007). Gradations in digital inclusion: Children, young people and the digital divide. New Media & Society, 9(4), 671–696. https://doi.org/10.1177/1461444807080335

Ng, W. (2012). Can we teach digital natives digital literacy? Computers & Education, 59(3), 1065–1078. https://doi.org/10.1016/j.compedu.2012.04.016

Odgers, C. L., & Jensen, M. R. (2020). Annual Research Review: Adolescent mental health in the digital age: Facts, fears, and future directions. Journal of Child Psychology and Psychiatry, 61(3), 336–348. https://doi.org/10.1111/jcpp.13190

Radesky, J. S., Schumacher, J., & Zuckerman, B. (2015). Mobile and interactive media use by young children: The good, the bad, and the unknown. Pediatrics, 135(1), 1–3. https://doi.org/10.1542/peds.2014-2251

Ribble, M. (2012). Digital citizenship in schools: Nine elements all students should know (2nd ed.). ISTE.

Twenge, J. M. (2017). iGen: Why today's super-connected kids are growing up less rebellious, more tolerant, less happy—and completely unprepared for adulthood. Atria Books.

11

Maintaining Balance — Raising Healthy Children in a Digital World

"Balance is not something you find; it's something you create." Jana Kingsford

As parents, we often find ourselves navigating the push and pull of technology. On one hand, it offers incredible opportunities for learning, connection, and creativity. On the other hand, it poses challenges that can feel overwhelming — from digital media addiction to privacy concerns, from social pressures to mental health risks.

But here's the good news: You are not powerless in this digital landscape. The secret to raising healthy, happy children in a tech-driven world lies in balance. By creating a healthy, mindful approach to technology, you can equip your child with the skills they need to thrive, not just survive, in a digital world.

In this final chapter, we'll recap the essential principles for raising children in the digital era, provide strategies for maintaining balance, and offer tips for fostering a positive, healthy relationship with technology for both you and your child.

Setting the Foundation: The Role of Parents in Shaping Digital Habits

It starts with you. As a parent, you are the role model for your child. The way you engage with digital media — how you manage your time, how you respond to digital distractions, and how you communicate about digital media — shapes their behavior.

KEY POINTS TO REMEMBER:

Model Healthy Digital Media Use

Be mindful of your habits. Your child is always watching, and your actions set the tone for their approach to technology.

Set Boundaries for Yourself

Just as you encourage limits for your child, apply those same principles to your own screen time. Show them the importance of balance by setting your screen-time guidelines.

Engage in Digital Media-Free Time:

Make family activities a priority, from dinner without devices to weekend outings without phones. Create moments that foster connection, communication, and mindfulness away from the screen.

Building Digital Literacy and Critical Thinking

Your child's relationship with technology needs to be more than just knowing how to use it. They need to think critically about the content they encounter, recognize digital risks, and become mindful, respectful digital citizens.

KEY STRATEGIES:

Educate on Digital Literacy

Teach your child how to evaluate online content, question sources, and spot misinformation.

Discuss Digital Ethics

Focus on topics such as online kindness, privacy protection, and the importance of authenticity.

Encourage Problem-Solving with Digital Media

Allow your child to experiment with technology by creating digital projects. This builds creativity and critical thinking while fostering a healthy relationship with screens.

Mental and Emotional Health in the Digital Age

The digital world can affect your child's mental health if they aren't equipped with the right tools to navigate it. Digital pressures, cyberbullying, and social comparisons can take a toll on your child's self-esteem and well-being.

KEY STRATEGIES:

Promote positive social media habits

Help your child understand the "highlight reel" effect and the difference between real life and online life. Teach them to follow accounts that uplift them and unfollow those that bring them down.

Encourage face-to-face socializing

Limit the time your child spends on digital communication and prioritize face-to-face interactions to strengthen real-life relationships.

Support Emotional Resilience

Teach your child how to bounce back from digital challenges, such as online drama or negative feedback, and encourage self-care to protect their emotional well-being.

Screen Time and Sleep: Creating Healthy Habits

Excessive digital media use, particularly before bed, disrupts sleep patterns. Sleep is critical for both physical and cognitive development, and poor sleep can lead to irritability, lack of focus, and poor academic performance.

KEY STRATEGIES:

Set Screen Time Limits

Establish clear rules around screen time, especially before bedtime. Encourage digital-free time an hour before sleep to help your child wind down.

Promote a Healthy Sleep Routine

Create a bedtime routine that doesn't involve digital media, like reading, journaling, or listening to calming music. This will signal to your child's brain that it's time to relax and prepare for sleep.

Use Technology for Sleep Tracking: Help your child use apps that track sleep patterns, reinforcing the importance of healthy sleep habits.

Encouraging Offline Activities and Hobbies

Children need time away from digital media to reconnect with the world around them. Encouraging hobbies and activities outside of the digital realm is crucial to their development.

KEY STRATEGIES:

Explore New Activities

Encourage your child to explore hobbies that don't involve technology, whether it's drawing, playing a musical instrument, or getting involved in sports.

Make Time for Outdoor Play

Nature offers a perfect environment for children to learn, grow, and exercise. Encourage outdoor adventures and unstructured play to promote physical and emotional well-being.

Set Digital Media-Free Zones

Create spaces in your home where digital media is off-limits, such as the dinner table or bedrooms. Use these zones to encourage conversation and quality time without distractions.

Involving Your Child in Digital Decisions

As your child grows older, it's important to include them in decisions about their digital technology use. This empowers them to take responsibility for their screen time and develop healthy habits.

KEY STRATEGIES:

Create Screen Time Agreements Together

Sit down with your child and discuss acceptable limits for screen use. Allow them to have a say in the rules, making it more likely they'll respect the boundaries.

Encourage Open Dialogue

Make sure your child feels comfortable talking to you about their online experiences, including any challenges they face. Encourage open discussions about anything that concerns them.

Check in Regularly

Keep track of your child's digital media use without being intrusive. Set regular check-ins to discuss how they're feeling about their screen time and if they have any issues they'd like to address.

Conclusion: Raising Balanced Digital Citizens

The digital world is here to stay. As parents, the best thing you can do is help your child navigate it mindfully, building the skills and habits they need to thrive. Encourage curiosity, foster digital literacy, and emphasize the importance of balance.

By creating clear guidelines, modeling healthy behaviors, and prioritizing face-to-face connection, you're giving your child the foundation they need to become a confident, resilient digital citizen. They'll not only survive in this tech-driven world but flourish in it, using technology as a tool to enhance their lives rather than dominate them.

Keep in mind, technology itself isn't good or bad — it's our choices that make the difference. With the right balance, your child can enjoy the benefits of the digital world while maintaining a healthy and fulfilling offline life.

Final Thoughts

As we close this book, know that there is no perfect formula for managing technology in your child's life. It's a journey that requires patience, flexibility, and ongoing reflection. Keep the lines of communication open, continue to educate yourself, and stay committed to helping your child develop a healthy relationship with the digital world.

After all, the most important thing is not how much time your child spends in front of a screen, but how they use that time — to learn, grow, and become the best version of themselves in an ever-evolving digital landscape.

References

American Academy of Pediatrics. (n.d.). *Screen time affecting sleep*. Retrieved from https://www.aap.org/en/patient-care/media-and-children/center-of-excellence-on-social-media-and-youth-mental-health/qa-portal/qa-portal-library/qa-portal-library-questions/screen-time-affecting-sleep/Home

Digital Wellness Lab. (n.d.). *How do I model good digital media and tech habits for my kids?*. Retrieved from https://digitalwellnesslab.org/articles/how-do-i-model-good-digital-media-and-tech-habits-for-my-kids/The Digital Wellness Lab

Hally Health. (2023, May). *Kid's corner: How screen time affects kids' sleep*. Retrieved from https://hally.com/2023/05/kids-corner-how-screen-time-affects-kids-sleep/Hally Health

KidsSafe. (2023, October 27). *Maintaining a healthy balance between online and offline activities*. Retrieved from https://kidssafe.lk/2023/10/27/balancing-act-effective-screen-time-management-for-kids/Kids Safe

NCFE Schools. (2025). *Balancing screen time and offline activities for children*. Retrieved from https://ncfeschools.com/blog/balancing-screen-time-and-offline-activities-for-childrenNCFE Bangalore

New York Post. (2025, May 6). *Parents' obsessive technology use may have serious long-term effects on babies and toddlers: Study*. Retrieved from https://nypost.com/2025/05/06/lifestyle/parents-obsessive-technology-use-may-have-serious-long-term-effects-on-babies-and-toddlers-study/New York Post

Raising Children Network. (n.d.). *Parents & screen time: Role-modelling*. Retrieved from https://raisingchildren.net.au/grown-ups/family-life/media-technology/parent-technology-useRaising Children Network

U.S. Department of Homeland Security. (n.d.). *Media literacy and critical thinking online*. Retrieved from https://www.dhs.gov/sites/default/files/publications/digital_media_literacy_1.pdfU.S. Department of Homeland Security

Webwise. (n.d.). *Digital literacy skills: Critical thinking*. Retrieved from https://www.webwise.ie/uncategorized/critical-thinking-digital-world/

www.ingramcontent.com/pod-product-compliance
Lightning Source LLC
LaVergne TN
LVHW060452061126
851857LV00016B/1803
* 9 7 9 8 3 8 5 1 3 0 3 5 1 *